SHE

IS

YOURS

JONATHAN AND WYNTER PITTS

HARVEST HOUSE PUBLISHERS
EUGENE, OREGON

Cover design by Connie Gabbert Design + Illustration

SHE IS YOURS
Copyright © 2017 by Wynter Pitts and Jonathan Pitts
Published by Harvest House Publishers
Eugene, Oregon 97402

www.harvesthousepublishers.com

ISBN 978-0-7369-7037-2 (pbk)
ISBN 978-0-7369-7038-9 (eBook)

Library of Congress Cataloging-in-Publication Data
Names: Pitts, Jonathan, author. | Pitts, Wynter, author.
Title: She is yours / Jonathan and Wynter Pitts.
Description: Eugene, Oregon : Harvest House Publishers, [2017]
Identifiers: LCCN 2017008141 (print) | LCCN 2017026292 (ebook) | ISBN
  9780736970389 (ebook) | ISBN 9780736970372 (pbk.)
Subjects: LCSH: Parenting—Religious aspects—Christianity. | Child
  rearing—Religious aspects—Christianity. | Girls. | Girls—Religious life.
Classification: LCC BV4529 (ebook) | LCC BV4529 .P58 2017 (print) | DDC
  248.8/45—dc23
LC record available at https://lccn.loc.gov/2017008141

Printed in the United States of America

18 19 20 21 22 23 24 25 / BP-SK / 10 9 8 7 6 5 4 3

CONTENTS

I prayed for this child, and the LORD answered my prayer.
He gave me this child. And now I give this child to the LORD.
He will serve the LORD all his life.

1 SAMUEL 1:27-28 ERV

NICE TO MEET YOU

Daughters. We know them well because we have four of our own. With more than 13,505 combined days of parenting girls under our belts, we can honestly say that raising Alena, Kaitlyn, and our twins Camryn and Olivia has dramatically changed our world… for the better!

Parenting a houseful of girls has caused us to take a deeper look at why God gave these special girls to us and how He intends us to operate as His children and their parents.

Our experience of raising four daughters with Jesus at the center of our world propelled us to write this book. Our girls are very different from each other, and each of them has a distinct personality—and that gives us much joy! However, we have had to experiment and learn, to try and try again, grappling with what it looks like to parent each of them while holding on to the values and the kingdom mindset befitting a family following after the heart of God.

In case you're wondering about the title of this book, it's really simple. "She is Yours" is a mindset. It is a constant reminder that everything we have is God's, including our daughters. Parenting from this perspective gives us purpose, identifies our responsibility, and defines our way of life.

We are raising God's girls, and because you are reading this book, we assume you are too.

She is yours—but she is also His.

God has created your daughter for a specific purpose. And He created you to parent her in a way that leads her heart and mind to His truth, love, and perfect will.

Sounds simple enough, right?

Wrong.

It did not take long for us to realize that raising our daughters was not going to be easy. If our daughters were robots and we could program them to think and act just the way we instructed them, then life with them would be a breeze. But they are not robots.

Girls are complex. They are tender yet strong, emotional but sturdy, and an inquisitive mix of facts and opinions. There are times when our task as parents of daughters makes total sense—and times when we can't seem to make sense of it at all!

So before we wrote the first word on these pages, we thought long and hard about how we should even begin. On some days it seemed wisest to ask you to join us on a treasure hunt, digging deep into the beautiful layers of raising daughters. There are so many gems to be found if only we take the time to pursue them.

Think about it. From the first years of toothless grins and endless giggles to the later seasons of messy hair buns and late-night conversations, there is no doubt that raising daughters is one of God's ways to reveal pieces of our hearts that we would otherwise never know existed.

Vulnerability, innocence, joy, spontaneity…these are all wrapped up in the four-letter word that describes our daughters: G-i-r-l.

However, let's not fool ourselves. There have been other days when it only seemed fitting that we would start the book by admitting that parenting girls is hard.

Our precious daughters have a unique way of exposing places in our hearts that we wish we could pray away.

There are moments when the giggles quickly give way to tears, the hugs turn into crossed arms, the discussions become a battle of wills, and we are left with feelings of anger, fear, frustration, and exhaustion, wondering what happened to our little girls and how it all happened so fast.

We don't doubt that you can relate to both scenarios, and before we go any further, we want you to know that we get it. We are not always overflowing with joy. Nor will we stop you to tell you how full your hands are and how difficult the upcoming years are going to be.

On the other hand, we will gladly sit down with you over your drink of choice and a warm piece of buttery bread (or in Jonathan's case, a box of Hot Tamales) to compare notes. We will hug you when she won't, and we will giggle with you over her most recent discoveries in her imaginary world. Just like you, we see and appreciate the beauty and the challenges in both the tears and the laughter.

So how should we start our time together? Let's start with this: Parenting God's girls is a journey. We'd like to invite you to join us on ours.

We started this parenting journey as 24-year-olds, married almost a year. By the time we were 29, we found ourselves fumbling along with a brilliant 5-year-old, potty training a 2-and-a-half-year-old, and barely surviving life with two brand-new infant twins who refused to sleep—and they were *all girls*.

We found ourselves surrounded by four daughters and wondering, "How did we get here?" Our lives were chaotic in those early days—and often still are.

There is no denying that raising daughters is a big job that requires all hands on deck. But our responsibility as parents is much greater than serving chicken nuggets, finding shin guards, and counting heads as they enter and exit our minivans.

Our hands are full with much more than those temporal responsibilities because we have the gift, honor, and pleasure of being the heart, hands, and feet of Jesus to those around us—starting with our own girls. Raising Christ-loving, world-changing daughters of God is what we are striving to do.

"The Father has loved us so much! This shows how much he loved us: We are called children of God. And we really are his children. But the people in the world don't understand that we are God's children, because they have not known him."

1 JOHN 3:1 ERV

And though our hands are full with our responsibilities, we are well aware of the fact that these girls will never fully belong to us. We hold them with an open hand. We hug them tight but hold them loose because they ultimately belong to the One who made them and has them in the palm of His hand as well. He is their Creator, who loves them and who has great plans for their lives!

So we do not own them, but we are responsible to be their parents. What we do with the gifts God has given us will make a difference in our world for generations to come. As the perfect parent, God is our example.

If we are doing our job as parents (which includes plenty of hard work and sacrifice), our girls will readily connect with us as Mom and Dad. As they know and experience us in our sacrifice and in our work, their relationship with us will become secure, and they will know they are loved.

Likewise, the verse above is saying that as they know God,

experiencing Him in His sacrifice and His work, our girls will come to know that they are God's children and that they are loved by Him.

So God has given us not only our beautiful daughters but also an awesome responsibility. We are the primary tools God wants to use to introduce Himself and His love to our girls.

Whether you are a mother or a father, whether you are struggling with your first infant, raising busy toddlers, surviving a houseful of teens, navigating the roads of young adulthood, or a combination of all these…parenting girls is not an easy job, and it needs your full attention and presence. It requires a level of patience you may not have known existed and a prayer life you've probably always wanted to attain.

We want to encourage you to embrace your journey with your daughter, and we want to help you understand and appreciate your high calling. This journey is about intentionally leading your daughter to the everlasting love of her Creator. And it's about seeking God, recognizing that as a parent, you desperately need His guidance.

As we consider our responsibility to God and our life with our girls, we will focus on three areas:

- In part 1, we'll look at her relationship with God.

- In part 2, we'll talk about her relationship with you.

- In part 3, we'll address her relationship with the world around her.

All three parts are designed to help you continue your journey of trusting God with the girl He gave you and to help you own your responsibility to steward her heart, mind, and soul.

We are so glad our paths have crossed. It's nice to meet you, and we look forward to becoming friends. Let's start our journey together by acknowledging the Lord's ownership of what is already His.

——————————— LET'S PRAY ———————

Dear God,

I release my daughter into Your care.

> I surrender my desire to control her.
> I surrender my desire to manipulate her future.
> I surrender my tendency to overprotect, shelter, and suffocate her.
> I surrender my desire to be her best friend, first.
> I surrender my own dreams for her.
> I surrender my need to be her source.

She is Yours.

I'm totally open to You, dependent on You, and desperate for You to be in control as I let go. I'm relying on the fact that You are God and that You have created my daughter for Your purpose and for this time.

> I pray that You will draw her to Yourself.
> I pray that she will delight in You.
> I pray that You will be patient with her.
> I pray that You will provide for her.
> I pray that You will bless her.
> I pray that You will use her to be a blessing to others.
> I pray that You will mature her.
> And ultimately, I pray that she will show Jesus in her very being.

I trust in Your sovereignty. I wait in expectation for Your providence.

Lord, she is Yours, and I trust You with her.

Amen.

PART 1

HER
RELATIONSHIP
WITH GOD

HER RELATIONSHIP WITH GOD—LET'S GET STARTED

Over the years of parenting our girls, one of the most useful pieces of advice we've received is from our pediatrician. Without fail, toward the end of every visit, he says, "Now remember: You can't control whether your kids will eat, but you can control the options available to them."

Although this piece of advice is about encouraging our daughters to eat a well-balanced diet, we think the words ring true in other circumstances—including how we approach their relationship with God.

We can't force our daughters to have a relationship with their Creator, but we can surround them with the evidence of His love and opportunities to partake in His truth. As parents, we can control how much time we spend with the Lord as a family and commit to renewing our minds with His strength.

At initial glance, this may seem like a daunting task. You might think, "I don't have the time," or "I don't want to bore my kids," but I promise you that both of those thoughts are distractions from what the Lord wants to do through you and your girls. Whether you practice family prayers in the mornings before school, lead a dinnertime Scripture reading and prayer (devotions), or share the day's highs and lows at bedtime, we encourage you to be intentional in your efforts. Help everyone in your family to experience a renewed mind.

Allocating time to spend with God together is crucial. Our girls will imitate our actions, and they need examples of what spiritual exercise looks like. Sunday school is not enough because corporate worship is naturally geared toward corporate growth. Personal growth must be modeled at home.

There is no getting around the fact that God's plan for your daughter involves *your* relationship with God, *your* commitment to His Word, and *your* preparation for each day of her life. The Lord has given our family some of the sweetest moments together when we've intentionally spent time renewing our minds and aligning our wills with His.

We are committed to growing in God's Word personally and demonstrating through example how our daughters can live out God's perfect will for them.

This lesson requires more than teaching. Our example is just as crucial as taking them to the Bible. If you're taking them to God's Word but not living it yourself, they will see hypocrisy. It is critical for what you do and what you say to be in alignment. As a child of God yourself, you are His image bearer. The degree that your life—your attitudes and actions—reflects the character of God will be the degree to which they experience what the love of God looks like. Your life is a litmus test for your girls of whether God's Word is true, real, and worth applying to their lives.

Don't let this reality scare you. It sometimes scares us because our initial reaction is to remember all the mistakes we've made. We will make similar mistakes tomorrow, next week, next year—or even in the next hour! But the good news of the gospel is that there is always grace. Leading our girls to the truth of the gospel means teaching them about the grace of God, which Jesus brought through His life, burial, and resurrection. It also means modeling that grace. Our leadership should include humbly, transparently, and authentically seeking God's grace as we fail Him, as well as seeking grace when we fail our girls. Leadership includes extending that same grace to them, remembering that without grace we would not be where we are today.

In each chapter, it is our hope that you learn something new about God, His Word, yourself, or your daughter that will benefit you on this journey. Even more earnestly, we pray you will apply what you learn or what the Holy Spirit reveals so that your daughter's relationship with God may be enhanced by what she observes in your life.

1

HER PREPARATION

WYNTER | I have a vivid memory of being a new bride, sitting on our sky-blue sofa and making the call to tell Jonathan we were pregnant. The call went something like this.

Me: Hey! You are not going to believe this…

Jonathan: What is it?

Me: Well, you know how I haven't been feeling well?

Jonathan: Mm-hm.

Me: Well, today my aunt told me she had a dream about a beautiful, curly-haired baby girl with big brown eyes…You know what that means, right?

Jonathan: [silence]

Me: It means someone in the family is pregnant…

Jonathan: [silence]

Me: It's us! I took a test!

Jonathan: Whoa, babe!

[A few moments of nervous laughter, followed by more silence.]

Jonathan: Okay, let me go. I just started a round.

Me: Huh? You're just going to keep golfing?

Jonathan: Yep…I mean, well, I was…Okay, I'll just play nine.

Me: Yeah, good idea.

Now, many years later, we laugh at this exchange often. But let me be honest: The longer I sat alone on that couch while Jonathan finished his round of golf, the more I wondered if God had made a mistake. Better yet, I wondered why we had let this happen. It was not the plan.

JONATHAN | Wynter is referring to a phone conversation that took place just two short months after we'd said "I do." It also happened to be two weeks after our college graduation.

Our goal was to get married while keeping in step with everything our peers were doing. We had a five-year plan. I can't help but laugh as I write this because our plan was to settle down, climb the corporate ladder, build wealth, and travel the world together before adding children to our lives. Getting pregnant right after we got married was not our plan.

Needless to say, I am so grateful for our lack of planning ability in this particular area. Had our plans played out, our lives would look drastically different. Instead of climbing ladders, we celebrated our first wedding anniversary with a three-month-old baby girl. Our second baby girl arrived two and a half years later, and a set of fraternal twin girls just two and a half years after that!

So, here we are. Four girls in all.

At one point or another, you realize that parenting is a charge you are completely unprepared for. Thankfully, no matter how adequate or inadequate we feel, God has graciously given us His Word as a template. We have an example to follow as we prepare to raise the daughters He gave us.

WYNTER | When I think of the word "prepare," my mind immediately drifts back to one of my earliest memories of the biblical character John the Baptist. This is probably because when I was a little girl, his was the loudest voice in my church's Easter play. The chosen male actor would march right down the dimly lit middle aisle and loudly proclaim, "Prepare ye the way of the Lord!" Year after year I grew to expect his entrance, but year after year his gruff and sudden appearance caused me to jump. His loud voice sent a tiny vibration through my chest, and as he marched, he would choose faces from the audience to look at directly while delivering his message.

At that age, I doubt I had ever read John's words written in the Gospels, but each year I anticipated hearing them—"Prepare ye the way of the Lord!" I was drawn to the character, his appearance, his sound, and his words.

So with my eyes wide, I would sit on the edge of my seat and watch as he moved with purpose toward the front of the auditorium. The bright light would shine on him as he stood alone, yet surrounded by the crowd that was already in place. This is when I would get my best visual of John the Baptist.

He never looked like the other characters in the play. His clothing was not colorful; it was plain and tattered. His voice was neither celebratory nor joyful; instead, it was boisterous and sharp. The hair on his head and on his face was unkempt, and it was obvious that he chose to focus on more important matters.

Quite frankly, he was odd.

Yet somehow, despite the discomfort that his oddity caused, the weight of his message captivated the attention of all who heard it.

Now, I do not claim that my church's portrayal of John the Baptist is 100 percent accurate. However, the truth of his message commanded my attention then and does so even more today.

As parents, we are called to prepare the way for God to work in the lives of those He has gathered around us—especially our children.

If your wide-eyed daughter has ever stared at you and wondered why you seemed so odd, then maybe it is because you, too, have made your way to the front of the crowd. Maybe you are standing in the light and commanding her attention with a message of truth.

I want you to know that you are not alone, and that you are doing what God has asked you to do.

Now, don't worry. If you have never felt odd or awkward in front of your daughter, just be patient. Seek God's truth and choose to live by it. Causing discomfort, speaking truth boldly, and standing alone in the crowd are all parts of this journey of preparing the way for God to work in her life.

In preparing the way for our girls, we are to make ready and create an environment where the love and truth of Jesus Christ may flourish in their hearts.

On the contrary, to prepare does not mean to manipulate, force, or craft a plan that will ensure the success, safety, and salvation of our daughters. As tempting as it is to try, that is their Creator's job.

We have a job, but we do not have ownership. John the Baptist's job was to prepare the way for those who were in need of Jesus's gift of salvation, and so is ours. Of course, we have many tasks to complete, but all those tasks revolve around the fact that Jesus Christ should be central in our lives and in the lives of our girls.

Jonathan and I were both fortunate to grow up in homes where the Bible was more than coffee-table decor. Rather, the words were woven into every detail of our lives. Like it or not—and most days it was "not" for me as a child—this was a reality, and it has shaped my life and the way we parent our girls today.

As you can imagine, this was not ideal when I was a selfish five-year-old who did not want to share my dolls. Being raised solely by my mother, I spent a considerable amount of time with my grandparents. Thankfully, despite my father's absence, his parents were still very much in the picture. My grandmother in particular was always quick to tell me when I was not being nice and when God was not pleased with my actions. "Do to others as you would like them to do to you" (Luke 6:31 NLT) played on repeat for most of my young years.

Later, as a college student, I remember calling my mother in tears because I was lonely. My mother did not coddle me with her words, but she shared the importance of trusting God's timing and being a good steward of the season I was in by spending my lonely days seeking Him. All I really wanted was for her to pray that God would send me a boyfriend! Instead she chose to push me toward the Bible.

I quickly learned that if I didn't want to know what the Bible had to say on a matter, I shouldn't present my problems to my family. God's Word was at the core of everything they said and did. They relied on the Bible and pointed to God's view in all situations. What we listened to, what we watched, and how and with whom we spent our time were brushed against the Bible and how it applied to the details of life.

And it did not stop in my home. Whenever possible, my mother invited our friends, our neighbors, and—much to my embarrassment—random strangers from the local grocery store into our walk with Christ.

As a child, I remember my mother gathering me, my brother, and a group of neighborhood kids to study the Bible and talk about the way it related to the issues we faced daily. We met on Mondays, so we creatively named it Monday Night Bible Study. (I know, very original!) On most of those Monday nights, I also remember being annoyed. Being the youngest in the group, all I wanted to understand was why it was taking me so long to grow up!

Looking back now, I'm so grateful for my mother. Not once did she ignore or dismiss our actions, thoughts, or conversations as trivial. On those Mondays and throughout the week, as we gathered in our small dining room, she affirmed each of us in God's love and assured us that there was nothing in the Bible that was not meant for us.

Yes, I remember being annoyed, but I can't ignore my very vivid memories of Monday nights. My mother's diligence and her commitment to truth are important reasons why Jonathan and I now gather our own girls to make sure they, too, understand truth and practice holding to its standard. I never want my girls to think that God's Word does not apply to them. So no matter how difficult it is to schedule, we find time to study together.

As adults, you and I may not speak the same language as our daughters. They don't think the way we think, and they don't necessarily care about the things we care about. They oftentimes don't even think we "get it." However, their Creator "gets" them—because He created them. He has things He wants to tell them, such as why He cares about their friendships, their outfits, and even their science tests.

I realize there will be times when their beliefs will be challenged by peers, teachers, and others. However, like my own mother, I am committed to sacrificing my time, convenience, and comfort to make sure their lives are drenched in truth.

My prayer is that their understanding of, belief in, and reliance on God's Word would be so ingrained that their consciences would automatically detect the lies that will inevitably come their way.

JONATHAN | Wynter's childhood was different from mine in many ways, but the high regard given to God's Word was a mirrored value. God's Word was taken as truth, and I couldn't go far without running into the implications of that reality. It affected how I related to the Creator of the universe and the people around me.

We have already mentioned the word "truth" quite a few times, so let's define what we mean. The truth is what God says about anything. Every single page of the Bible has truth written all over it.

Basic truths are things you really don't have to teach your children. For example, you don't have to teach your children that it's wrong to hit. They have a built-in moral compass that exposes this offense before you have a chance to even correct it. It might not keep them from doing it, but it will most definitely bring shame.

Even this very fact is found in Scripture. Romans 1:20 says, "God's eternal power and character cannot be seen. But from the beginning of creation, God has shown what these are like by all he has made" (CEV).

So no, you don't have to teach your daughter that there is a right and a wrong. Catch even a one-year-old doing the wrong thing, and you will see her trying to cover it up.

My family was not perfect by any means, but we were committed to God's Word. In fact, if you came into my home, you couldn't avoid the face of Jesus. His picture was literally hanging on our walls! But even more than that, He was at our table when my mom or dad led us in family devotions. He was in our prayers at breakfast, lunch, and dinner, before we left for school, before we went to bed, and any other time we needed to call on Him. And He was in every single parental discipline confrontation.

Before you start thinking my parents were "Bible-thumping fundamentalists," let's get one thing straight. They were and they still are, but not in a negative way. You see, my parents' lives were changed by the gospel of Jesus Christ. His love shaped their marriage, their family, and everything they did in life. It still does. Their imperfect lives, glued together with the love of God, created a light for my path.

I continue to thank God for my parents with all my heart. With all they could muster, they made sure that I tasted God's goodness, and that I experienced His love and grace in the good times and bad times (of which there were plenty).

Our family stuck out like a sore thumb in rural South Jersey. My mom is a Midwestern German, and my father is a Northeastern African-American. In a time when being an interracial couple was unpopular at best, they were also raising a Christian family. I distinctly remember arguments in high school and college with friends who adamantly disagreed with marriage between races, specifically between black and white. Some of them even used Scripture to support their view, albeit out of context.

On top of this social challenge, we had financial difficulties. My parents were both hard workers, but they had five kids. This meant that my mother spent most of her time at home. Once we were all in school, she was able to teach at a small Christian school, but the income was small. For most of our childhood, my father moved from one job to the next. The 1980s economy wasn't the strongest, and we struggled. I never remember missing a meal, but we did split a candy bar five ways on more than one occasion! Through it all, my parents made sure we knew that God was our provider and that His Word was our primary source of guidance.

Their faith wasn't dependent on positive circumstances. I witnessed consistent, prayerful, submissive, and intentional discipleship of Jesus Christ in their everyday lives. This doesn't mean they were perfect. It only means that they ran toward Jesus. When things went well, they praised the Lord. When things went badly, they sought the Lord and still praised Him. They were fully dependent on God and fully accountable to His Word. I saw a joy in their hearts as they served the Lord, and that joy was their strength.

I'm thankful my parents believed Psalm 34:8, which says, "Taste and see that the LORD is good; blessed is the one who takes refuge in him." Because of their faith, I tasted the goodness of the Lord. I watched my parents follow Jesus with their actions, not just with their words. One of the greatest takeaways from my childhood was experiencing the grace and love of God personally, leaving little doubt in my mind regarding its truth.

Following our families' examples, Wynter and I are committed to digging our heels into God's Word and evaluating our lives against its truth. As you already know, we do not do it perfectly, but we try. Around the dinner table, sprawled out on a bed, or sitting around the living room floor, we worship together, open God's Word, and take turns reading and discussing what He is saying to us as often as we can. We want to be well equipped to live it out, first with our girls and then with everyone else who crosses our path.

WYNTER | Jonathan is right: The time we spend together growing in God's Word is one of the most consistent pieces of our family puzzle. We value it and we treasure it. That said, you should know that our time together is laced with chaos more often than not. Just picture it—four girls, two parents, a dog, and the Bible. We have experienced every form of pandemonium you can imagine. I don't even feel the need to go into details here—just let your imagination run wild!

Regardless of what it looks like, taking the time to seek Christ together and grow your family in His truth must start with your willingness to do the work.

I remember one day when our middle daughter, Kaitlyn, was six years old. She was tucked away in her room playing alone. Suddenly I heard her call out for me to come.

In a panic, I rushed to her and found her sitting proudly in front of a new puzzle she had just completed. "Mommy, Mommy—look how fast I can put this puzzle together!" She was beaming.

In an effort to attain my full attention, she glanced up at me again and said two very familiar words: "Mommy, watch!"

I stood in the doorway and watched as she carefully flipped the puzzle over onto the floor, keeping each piece intact. Next she placed them, one by one, back onto the emptied puzzle board in the exact same order as she had flipped them. She completed the puzzle in a matter of seconds, and she was so proud.

By her definition, my sweet girl had definitely put the puzzle together at a record-breaking speed. However, by any other standard, what she did would not be considered praiseworthy.

In this moment, I found myself faced with a happy girl and an internal dilemma. I could simply congratulate her and rejoice in her "success," or I could ruin her excitement with a bit of truth. She had not succeeded. By taking the shortcut, she had cheated.

In all honesty, I thought long and hard about this one! She was happy with the job she did, and I was busy folding the first of six loads of laundry that had been blocking my doorway for five days. Walking away from this one would have been an easy response. "Does it really matter?" I thought.

I took a deep breath and decided it did. It mattered. I needed her to know that regardless of the details, I was committed to maintaining the standard.

I knelt down and explained to her why she didn't really break a record with the method she used. She was crushed, and she melted right before my eyes.

"But it's so hard that way, Mommy," she whimpered.

She was correct. Putting a puzzle together can be difficult. It takes patience and concentration. Many times it's simply trial and error when trying to figure out which piece fits where. However, to count a puzzle completion as a success, you have to start with the pieces completely disarrayed. That's the true definition of putting a puzzle together.

Here's what I learned about truth from this less-than-perfect example. We cannot lower the bar or change the rules when we are tired, preoccupied, or saddened by our daughter's disappointment. Whether the task is as simple as putting a puzzle together at six years old or a more complicated scenario—such as how to handle a teenager's dishonesty—our priority is bringing her to the standard of God's truth.

If we are committed to God's Word, we will challenge her to rise to a level of truth in all areas of her life now and pave a sure path for her to follow when she begins to walk alone.

JONATHAN | You may be thinking, "This is all great, but my childhood did not include Monday night Bible studies, family devotions, or pictures of Jesus on the wall."

Please know that we don't mention our childhoods to give credit or boast of some sort of advantage. We are far from perfect in our parenting and in our understanding and application of God's Word. We each have a journey and testimony of God's grace in our lives, and we will share more of that in the following chapters. Although our families planted God's truth in our hearts, there was still plenty of work to be done as we grew up—and there still is today. However, we are grateful for the examples that were set before us because they testify to the effectiveness and importance of establishing a family's roots in the Word of God.

If you are already actively using God's Word as the standard for your family, our prayer is that you continue. We pray you'll grow even deeper in God's Word—even amid the chaos that comes with it! If you have never considered using the Bible as your standard and measurement for truth, then we encourage you to begin. A good place to start is with a family time of devotions to God, spending a few minutes reading the Bible after a meal or before bedtime. It's never too late to start!

Keeping God's Word at the center of your life is essential to successful parenting. So let me ask you this: How committed are you
to doing the work of knowing God's Word and applying it to your
life? After all, leading others to Him is possible only if you seek and
follow Him yourself.

This is not a guilt trip. We ask ourselves this very question daily.
As parents, our passionate pursuit of a real and vibrant relationship
with Jesus has a direct impact on our ability to lead our daughters
to God's grace.

When creating an environment that welcomes God's presence,
we must rely on His Word—the Bible. Without it as our foundation, it's impossible to succeed—at anything!

Here are a few helpful tips.

- *If you have multiple children of varying ages, you can create a schedule, giving each child a turn to lead your time
  together.* This not only builds them up in God but also
  builds them up in patience, grace, and kindness for each
  other. Don't get frustrated if cooperation doesn't happen
  right away. We must admit that we are works in progress
  ourselves.

- *If you ever entertain guests or extended family, use it as an
  opportunity to invite them into the conversation.* We have
  found that our girls' interest is piqued when they get to
  hear about someone else's journey with God. It gives
  them a different perspective and reminds them that we
  aren't alone on this journey.

- *Get creative.* God has given you everything you need to
  succeed. It comes down to allocating time and attention and being willing to approach the table of hard-
  ship. Treat it like a workout. Everyone works out a little

differently, depending on their preferences. Spiritual exercise is no different.

- *Have fun.* Worshipping and spending time with God can be fun. Yes, learning can seem boring, and routines can start to feel old, so make sure you are doing things to inspire your daughters. Open their minds and captivate them. The options are limitless!

We encourage you to be consistent. Be committed. Be patient. Remember that God has not asked us to perfect our daughters before leading them to His grace. He has called us to create an environment where they see His grace lived out through us, in a way that lines up with His Word. Jesus entered the chaos for us, so we choose to enter the chaos with our girls.

─────────────── LET'S PRAY ───────────────

Father,

I know that You have called me to prepare the way for my daughter to know You. And I'll admit, sometimes this call seems overwhelming. On most days I don't feel prepared myself, much less ready to prepare her. So I come to You in full transparency, asking You to help me to do what I cannot. Remind me that I cannot do it on my own, nor are You asking me to.

Help me to own my role while relinquishing the results to You. Help me to continually use Your Word as the standard for all topics, and give me insight into Your Word that I might lead her to it. Holy Spirit, give me new insight and even favor with my daughter, that she might trust me. Give me creativity. Give me passion.

And help me to remember that knowing You should be fun and exciting. Thank You for trusting me with this incredible task, and lead me as I lead her.

She is Yours, and I trust You with her.

Amen.

2

HER KNOWLEDGE OF GOD

WYNTER | My grandfather, Two Daddy, is one of the most intriguing people I know. I say this with an overwhelming amount of love and gratitude. Before I was born, he made a bold decision to follow Christ, and as a result, his life changed mine. Christ laid the foundation in him for his wife and children to follow—a truth I didn't fully appreciate until adulthood. As a little girl, what stood out to me most were his quirky gestures, facial expressions, and signature statements.

I have always loved imitating him. In fact, if you and I were sitting face-to-face, here's how I would do it. I would place a hand on each knee, tilt my head a little, and begin swaying and whistling a medley of "Amazing Grace" or "How Great Thou Art." Then I would stop momentarily, clear my throat three times, blink quickly, and say, "Now…now…remember, don't take no wooden nickels."

If you have ever met a person who made you want to sit at their feet and listen, laugh, and learn, then you know what I'm talking about. That's my Two Daddy.

Just thinking about him brings a smile to my face. My heart is full of gratitude for his wisdom and his willingness to share it with anyone he meets.

He tells a story about visiting a church one day. A kind stranger walked up to him and said, "I know you! You are Arthur Evans!" To which my grandfather replied, "You don't know me. You know *of* me!"

He laughed, shook the man's hand, and introduced himself for the very first time.

This may sound like an interesting exchange, but if you knew my grandfather, you would understand the sincerity and wisdom behind his words and actions.

You see, the man was a friend of my uncle, and he had heard numerous stories about my grandfather. So by no fault of his own, Two Daddy did not know this man even existed until this brief chat. My grandfather was trying to convey that although there may have been an exchange of information on one end, there was an absolute lack of relationship between them. The man knew my grandfather's name, the names of his children, and no doubt a few other pieces of personal information, yet he remained a stranger until they had a face-to-face encounter.

The more I think about this story, the more I realize how accurately it represents what happens to children like Jonathan and me. As we've mentioned, we grew up in Christian homes and were drenched daily in God's Word. But would it be true for us to say that we have known God our entire lives?

Definitely not. It is true that I cannot remember a time in my life when I did not have knowledge of God. But there were definitely seasons of not knowing Him.

As my Two Daddy explained, there is a difference.

I am grateful for grandparents who laid a Christ-centered foundation and a mother who led by example. However, no matter how many Bible verses they taught me, prayers they prayed over me, worship songs we sang together, or Monday night Bible studies I sat through, there is one thing they just couldn't give me—*a relationship with Jesus.*

Knowledge of God and knowing God can lead to very different life experiences. I often wonder if my children are learning how to move from *knowledge* about God to a *relationship* with Him.

For a long time, I didn't.

I knew biblical principles and many stories from the Bible. However, I didn't always understand how they applied to my ten-year-old, little-girl life.

I knew that the Bible was God's Word. I did not know what it had to do with me.

I knew that God was the Creator of the world. I did not know Him as my Father.

I knew that God was holy. I did not know that He loved me even when I wasn't holy.

I knew that Christ died to save the world from sin. I did not know how to live as a forgiven sinner.

Despite my mother's best efforts, it never fully dawned on me that the great big God of the universe knew me, completely understood me, and wanted a relationship with me as a little girl—just as much as He did with the adults who told me about Him.

I am grateful for my family because the information I received about Him helped me to recognize His presence. But before I could say I knew Him, I had to meet Him face-to-face. Today, I think about this concept often as I parent our growing daughters. I pray that today, in this season of their lives, my girls are beginning a lifelong journey of knowing God.

JONATHAN | When I think about the difference between knowing about God and knowing Him personally, the apostle Paul comes immediately to mind.

Paul talks about having been "taken hold of," meaning that Jesus grabbed ahold of him at a certain point in his life. Think about what an amazing feeling it is to know that God has grabbed you in His grace and that He holds you securely.

Have you ever played the trust game? You close your eyes and fall backward, trusting that someone is there to catch you. If done incorrectly, you could land on the ground after floundering in the air and trying to keep yourself from disaster. However, if done correctly, there is only a moment of uncertainty before you feel the strength of someone's hands on your back and know you've been caught.

The relief you feel in that moment is what Paul is talking about. You feel it when you've been floundering about and suddenly experience the presence of God in your life. You feel confident that His grasp has completely changed your outcome. God's grasp of Paul completely changed the trajectory of his life, and he spent his remaining days seeking the hand of the One who had grabbed Him.

"My goal is to know Him and the power of His resurrection and the fellowship of His sufferings, being conformed to His death, assuming that I will somehow reach the resurrection from among the dead. Not that I have already reached the goal or am already fully mature, but I make every effort to take hold of it because I also have been taken hold of by Christ Jesus."

PHILIPPIANS 3:10-12 HCSB

I find much comfort in this! There is nothing I want more than to know that regardless of their floundering, my daughters are safe and secure when they fall toward Jesus.

I thank God daily that His hands have laid hold of each of my girls, and I encourage them daily to rest in the strength of His grasp.

I remember getting a glimpse into this one Sunday when Alena, our oldest daughter, was eight years old. She had just returned from her Christian summer camp the previous Saturday. She must have spent her time at camp missing Wynter and me, because she asked if she could stay in the worship service with us instead of going to Sunday school.

I don't remember the service being any different from most Sundays. Worship was great, and the pastor brought a great message, but it was nothing out of the ordinary—at least not from my human perspective. But as the service drew to its end, the pastor called on people to reaffirm their commitment to following Jesus. (Of course, this experience can look very different and often does, depending on the denomination and culture of a church. One of my greatest joys in life so far has been traveling the country and experiencing much of the church and its diversity, especially as it pertains to their specific calls to faith in Jesus Christ.)

Alena asked if I would take her forward. As a father who wants my girls to walk faithfully with the Lord, I gladly accepted her invitation. She had already asked Jesus to be her sin bearer and Savior, and she had committed her life to following Him. Knowing all this, I assumed she just had some extra things she wanted to commit to the Lord, and so we walked.

The pastor prayed a prayer of dedication for those who were giving their lives to Christ for the first time, as well as for those who wanted to double down in terms of their service to Him. It was in the middle of the prayer that I glanced over at Alena and saw her sobbing. Seeing my daughter cry was nothing new, but even at a glance, I could tell that something was different. She was crying with a deep inner cry that doesn't happen when your sister loses your favorite pencil or you've been told no to a playdate request. This cry came from deep within her soul. I recognized it because there was desperation, joy, and longing that I had once felt as a child and continue to feel whenever I recognize God's grace and my need for it anew.

Though familiar, it still caught me a bit off guard. As we walked to our seats after the prayer time, I put my arm around her and tried to comfort her. When we got back to our seats, she continued to cry, and I became concerned that there was an issue. So I asked, "Is everything okay? Are these sad tears or happy tears?"

She answered that her tears were happy tears. She continued to cry for the next ten minutes or so. It was an incredible moment to witness our daughter falling into the arms of her Father. It was as if she had previously made the decision mentally, and God, in His wisdom and perfect timing, flooded her heart with His mercy and grace in a way she had never experienced before. I believe this was a defining moment in her life, when she chose to move from knowledge of God into a whole new level of relationship with Him.

As parents, it was tempting to pat ourselves on the back for a job well done. We could have easily thought, "I'll take the credit for that one," or "We did it!" But we were sober-minded enough to remember that drawing hearts to His presence is the Lord's job, and that His call is just that—*His* call. It is His work alone. So instead of pride, our hearts were filled with gratitude for answered prayers.

More than anything else we have wanted our children to follow Jesus, so we've prayed that same prayer continually, desperately, over and over again. "Lord, thank You for Your grace and mercy. May our girls come to understand Your saving grace at an early age. And may they have a heart that longs for and chases after You." Okay, yes, it varies a bit from time to time, but not much. It is a simple request that we know only God can honor. Our prayer is that our daughters would know the Lord Jesus Christ in all His power and that, by faith, they may grab ahold of all that God has for them and seek daily to know Him more.

WYNTER | Knowing God should not be viewed as a box to be checked off, but a deep and ever-deepening experience of relationship with Jesus Christ. When thinking about your daughters and their relationship with Christ, remember that having knowledge of God and knowing Jesus are two different things. One cannot replace the other.

We are to continue presenting our daughters with information about God while demonstrating a life lived in relationship with Him. Personally, I wish there was a magic four-step program we could outline to ensure the smooth transition of information from head to heart. Unfortunately, nothing like that exists. Activities like studying God's Word as a family and participating in church and Bible memory activities have been important in our home, but ultimately, raising daughters to grow in relationship with Jesus begins with raising daughters who know God's Word, have tasted His goodness, and meet Him face-to-face.

I wholeheartedly believe that God's Word itself is enough to cause the heart change we all need. Here are a few practical ways to bring God's Word front and center:

- *Be the example.* Let her see you reading and hear you talking about God's Word in your daily life. Then let her see you living with authenticity, admitting when you fail and running toward Jesus for grace.

- *Pray for boldness and confidence with her and for her.* Your daughter needs to learn early that choosing to be like Christ will not always make her popular. In fact, it will often come with challenges. She will need God's strength as she gets to know and experience Him.

- *Help her to carve out time.* It is true that many things will not happen if we do not schedule them. Encourage your daughter to set aside time to dig into the Word of God and spend time with Him.

- *Use God's Word as a standard for living.* Study God's Word together and teach her how to apply it to her everyday situations. In times of joy, fear, disobedience, or encouragement, find Scriptures that apply. Encourage her to write and post biblical principles around the house and in her room.

LET'S PRAY

Heavenly Father,

Thank You for making relationship with You possible through Jesus, and for speaking Your salvation message so clearly through Your Word. Thank You that because of my relationship with Jesus, I have grace and mercy for each day that I live. Thank You for the ability to ask, plead, and beg You for those things that I believe You desire for my family and me.

Lord, that is exactly what I am doing right now. My daughter needs You!

"I will do whatever you ask in my name, so that the Father may be glorified in the Son. You may ask me for anything in my name, and I will do it."

JOHN 14:13-14

I ask in Jesus's name that You would chase my daughter down in her everyday, ordinary life, interrupting it as You see fit in order to woo her to You.

I plead with You to be patient with her as she tries to stand in her humanness, and gently break her so that she would come to the end of herself. Help her to realize her need for You and dependence on You at a very young age.

I beg You to do whatever it takes to bring her into relationship with You.

She is Yours, and I trust You with her.

In Jesus's name, amen.

3

HER GROWTH

WYNTER | I am sure this comes as no surprise, but even after God so clearly grabbed ahold of my daughter's heart, Alena was not perfect (and still isn't). Though they are all wonderful little "God girls," not one of our girls is perfect. As a matter of fact, year after year we send all our girls to camp, praying for another encounter like the one our oldest had. I am joking, but only a little!

We do pray that God will continue to reveal Himself to them from one level to the next. It was such a beautiful experience to witness, and we couldn't help but ask for more of that. But I am reminded of what the apostle Paul says about his relationship with Christ. He says in Philippians 3:8,10 (NASB), "I have suffered the loss of all things, and count them but rubbish so that I may gain Christ… that I may know Him and the power of His resurrection," meaning there is still much of God he doesn't know. I don't know about you, but it gives me great hope to know that Paul, one of the great men of the Bible, knows God but is still pleading to know God more!

The truth is, our daughters come home from camp year after year having experienced a week of Christ-filled worship, teaching, and fun, yet somehow none of them have come back having "arrived" at full spiritual maturity. Jonathan and I often laugh because it's during the two-hour drive home from camp that we see our girls at their worst. They are exhausted, which also means they are a bit cranky, weepy, impatient, and easily annoyed, mostly by each other. There have been times when the back of the van sounds a lot like a battlefield, and pillows, words, and tears are used freely to attack.

Just picture it. Jonathan and I have not seen them for an entire week. We eagerly wake up at six in the morning, get dressed, and get on the road to ensure a front-row seat at their camp's closing ceremony. Two hours later we arrive to see hundreds of children jumping, running, and singing praises to God. Our hearts are instantly full of gratitude, our eyes are watery, and with each song of praise they sing during their ceremony, the evidence of God's presence cannot be denied. We know that over the last seven days our girls and so many others have been forever changed. We watch a short video of them jumping off diving boards, riding horses, being hit with paintballs, and participating in all sorts of other adventurous activities. The program ends, and when the girls first see each other and us, they are thrilled! They wrap their arms around my neck and Jonathan's waist. They introduce us to their newest friends and immediately start sharing their individual highlights of the week. We say our goodbyes, collect all our items from the lost and found, and head to the van.

As the last sliding door closes, the first tear falls, soon followed by shouts of "Don't touch me," "It's my turn," and "Stop chewing so loudly!" It is one of the most notable downshifts in the history of downshifts! In their defense, they are suffering from extreme sleep deprivation.

For the first few minutes we are patient and understanding, but by the time we reach the end of the campground, we simply cannot take it! It becomes tempting to condemn or shame them for behaving in such an ungodly and ungrateful manner. After having such an awesome, intense, weeklong experience in God's presence, how dare they?

This only lasts for about 40 minutes, and then everyone is sound asleep. It is an emotionally exhausting time that repeats itself whenever sleep is scarce and quarters are tight. We have discovered that sleepiness reveals the imperfections of our girls in a very real way.

Please tell us we are not alone in thinking that this parenting journey would be so much easier if such ungrateful, selfish, and bothersome scenarios would just disappear! I wish my daughters would simply listen, obey, and remember the first time—and for the rest of their lives. Instead I often find myself in the middle of situations like these, when immediate correction and guidance are necessary.

Sometimes just waking up in the morning provokes mayhem and undesirable behaviors from my Christ-filled children! There have been days, weeks, and seasons when all I do is teach, redirect, and discipline over and over again while praying for some sign of progress. Or better yet, I pray for God Himself to force them into perfect behavior at once. Oh, how grateful I would be! Unfortunately, this is just not how it works.

I love to see my girls emotionally connecting with their Creator through prayers, worship, and even tears, but what I truly long to see are daily interactions that give evidence of growth.

Ironically, it is often when I'm correcting my daughters that I need the Lord's patience and encouragement myself. When I reach the point of complete frustration, God always graciously pulls me in close and reminds me of His love and grace.

As a matter of fact, He reminds me that not only is He always willing to correct when needed, but He does it because of His love for me.

Ouch.

I may not cry because I need a nap (actually, I just may), but I am certainly guilty of being impatient with those closest to me. I don't normally kick someone who touches my leg with their knee, but I'm not always gentle with my words, thoughts, or actions. In dealing with my girls' whining or their tantrums, I have often displayed anger and impatience.

"The Lord disciplines the one He loves, just as a father, the son he delights in."

PROVERBS 3:12 HCSB

Nothing better demonstrates the importance of needing God's grace than revealing our own needs to our children. When appropriate, I bring the girls into my world, letting them see that I am not perfect. I even go as far as describing the steps I am taking to change my attitude and heart. I realize I can tell my girls what the Bible says, but ultimately they will more likely follow the path I've walked in front of them.

God uses opportunities of discipline to correct and patiently pull us in the right direction. Regardless of our faults, He guides us deeper into relationship with Him. Thankfully, my actions do not cause Him to push me away. Instead, they draw Him in closer. He lets me taste the fruit of His Spirit, and He uses my times of weakness as opportunities to show me who He is.

Galatians 5:22-23 tells us that He is "love, joy, peace, forbearance, kindness, goodness, faithfulness, gentleness and self-control."

I see His kindness when I am angry. I experience His gentleness when I am harsh, and I feel His peace amid chaos and turmoil. He is consistent in the way that He loves. Oh, what a good Father He is to me and to you!

What would happen if our standard for correction looked like

His rather than an annoying recurrence of what didn't work yesterday? Our girls need to taste His fruit, and discipline should be viewed as an opportunity to lead by example and offer a taste of the very fruit we are praying they display.

Now, as I type this, I am fully aware of what a challenge this is. As I said at the beginning of this chapter, our girls are not angels, and we cannot recall any days when our response has been perfect. We are constantly apologizing and forever recalibrating. However, they are His children, and just like all of us, they are in need of more of His Spirit. Whether your girl is 8 months or 7, 16, or 22 years old, there is one thing that remains true: Like us, she is a work in progress. As a result, our discipline should look and feel like love.

Thankfully, God has provided just what is needed to parent the children He has given us. God's Word, the Bible, is not only a resource to correct ungodly children, but also a tool to encourage godliness. Scripture's purpose amid discipline is not to bring about guilt, but rather to affirm my girls in God's truth despite their action and my frustrations. This means I cannot simply quote verses like Ephesians 6:2 and say, "Doesn't the Bible say to honor your father and your mother?" Rather, in the midst of their correction, I should also encourage them with verses like Lamentations 3:22 (ESV): "The steadfast love of the LORD never ceases; his mercies never come to an end."

Lord,

Thank You for entrusting me with Your child. Help me to understand her more clearly. Teach me to be slow to anger, and help me to abound in love and faithfulness as I walk out Your compassion and grace in this situation. I need Your wisdom, words, and discipline.

Amen.

In moments of complete exhaustion and frustration, I want to remember that I am a work in progress and so are my children. God uses the imperfections of our growing girls to shine a light on our ongoing need for His grace in our own lives. My actions, my words, and my thoughts should look like His, especially when I am parenting the girls He gave me.

Let's not get so focused on her behavior, desirable or not, lest we forget what a gift we've been given to witness her growth. As parents, we have a front-row seat to watch His garden grow. When we see our girls struggling in a particular area, whether it be lacking in love, patience, kindness, joy, or other Christlike characteristics and behaviors, our responsibility and our pleasure is to water the fruit He has planted in their hearts. We should view our homes as the training ground for that very purpose. We have to trust and pray that God is doing what only He can do.

"Guard your heart above all else, for it is the source of life."

PROVERBS 4:23 HCSB

Friends, regardless of your daughter's knowledge of God and in spite of her emotions, her heart is her battlefield. What matters most is cultivating what happens in her heart. Perfect behavior from her is not the goal. Instead, love, joy, peace, patience, kindness, goodness, gentleness, faithfulness, self-control, and other Christlike attributes that come only from their proximity to Jesus—these are higher priorities. If I want to see evidence of growth in my daughter, then I have to patiently nurture her growth by leading her closer to Christ.

The enemy wants nothing more than to control her life, and his entry point is her heart. Our encouraging words, our loving actions, and our consistent behavior are vital to her growth, which is her main protection from the enemy.

I love the book of John. In the first few chapters, we get such a clear view of how Jesus personally interacted with those He met. Despite what their outward actions or words revealed, Jesus always looked to their hearts and offered them the fruit they needed.

Jesus was kind to Nicodemus when he questioned Him in John 3. He was patient with the straying woman at the well in John 4. He showed self-control when Judas betrayed Him. And He was loving to sinners like you and me when He sacrificed His life that we might live, as shown in John 3:16.

I'm committed to displaying the very characteristics of growth that will help my daughters desire the growth that God has for them.

JONATHAN | Thinking about my girls' spiritual growth makes me immediately think about their physical growth. I love watching their spiritual growth with the eyes of my heart, just as I watch their physical growth with my physical eyes.

One of the greatest things about parenting in this social-media-driven generation is being constantly reminded of how fast things change and how quickly our girls grow up. For a family that has moved 1,395 miles away from the closest grandparent, social media has been a positive tool for staying connected. There is nothing like being able to share even the most ordinary videos or pictures to warm grandparents' hearts for hours on end. They replay and share that special moment with their friends, experiencing as much pride as if they had been there in person.

We post new pictures, videos, and updates to our status on a regular basis. We even have apps that allow us to post to multiple social streams at once—making sure that no one misses out on the latest soccer game, dance recital, or random Saturday activity.

A few of these outlets also serve as great photo archives. Whenever we are looking for a few photos to frame or put in an album, social media is the first place we check. I literally cannot remember the last time I checked a digital camera or even my phone when looking for a photo or video memory. No, social media has become my first stop, and I'm typically not disappointed. The photos are sorted by source and date, so I usually can find exactly what I am looking for in just a few moments. It's truly amazing.

And it's the archive that spurred this thought.

I was sitting at my desk today, working away, when I stopped for a momentary break to check in on the social-media world. I know what you are thinking, but don't judge me! You've done it before, and you will do it again! Well, a "timeline photo" popped up—you know, the kind that pops up a year or five years after you first posted the photo.

The photo was of my oldest twin, Camryn, who was two at the time. She's our number three of the four girls. Well, the photo happened to be a five-year anniversary photo. The picture captured a somewhat normal view of her standing in a chair in my parents' church—the church where I grew up. We happened to be visiting New Jersey, during one of my twins' earliest trips to see their grandparents.

My first thought was, "I love that little face." She really was one of the cutest toddlers I have ever seen. She had a squishy little face that melted my heart, and to this very day it has the same effect.

My second thought was, "Man, she has grown up so fast!" Now, don't get me wrong—I have a good amount of time left with our girls in our home. But it was just yesterday that she was the squishy-faced little girl that showed up on my timeline.

My third thought was a bit more reflective, and it quickly aroused some anxiety. "My girls are growing so fast physically and emotionally, but are they growing spiritually?"

I have this thought quite frequently, which I take as an indication of the Spirit's work in my own life. I once heard it said that the first sign of spiritual maturity is questioning whether you are maturing at all. The concern and the discontentment are two of the Lord's ways of pushing us deeper into His will. My desire to disciple and train my girls in the things of the Lord is a sign of my desire to be a disciple. If you have this desire for your daughter, you can remove any anxiety from these thoughts by reminding yourself of God's grace.

As I think about my daughters' spiritual growth, I can't help but be overwhelmed at the enormous task that I have as a spiritual leader. But God's Word gives me hope.

When I think about 1 Corinthians 9:24, I think of myself as a track-and-field team captain. I imagine myself running a race, and my girls are my younger teammates. They are running behind me as I motivate them to finish strong, just as I finish strong. In other words, as a parent I'm challenged with the task of teaching my girls to run the race of faith. They are just a few strides behind me. As I run, they run. As I grow, they grow. My job is to motivate them with shouts of encouragement while letting my feet and my form do most of the talking.

"Do you not know that in a race all the runners run, but only one gets the prize? Run in such a way as to get the prize."
1 CORINTHIANS 9:24

Yes, I should be involved in making sure my girls are reading God's Word for themselves, but their first source of that knowledge should come from watching my routine. And yes, I should encourage them to pray routinely and "without ceasing," but their primary reminder should be seeing Wynter and me on our knees, praying with and over them, as well as praying for our neighbors, friends, and anyone the Lord brings to our minds. And lest they think our faith is focused only on our spiritual relationship with God, my girls should see me serving those who can't help themselves (widows and orphans). That is the truest form of our faith and the one that will lead our children down the path of victory in the race of faith.

Growth. Real growth doesn't happen naturally, unless you are talking about your daughter getting taller. No, spiritual growth happens as you exercise, as you train. As parents, instead of just telling our girls they need to grow, let's start by pursuing growth ourselves.

What if our goal was to get as fit as possible, taking them with us to the spiritual gym so they can watch us work out? What if we decided to "train [ourselves] to be godly" (1 Timothy 4:7) so that they might come to see the difference in our lives because of Christ?

"The fruit of the Spirit is love, joy, peace, forbearance, kindness, goodness, faithfulness, gentleness and self-control."

GALATIANS 5:22-23

Do you want your daughter to grow in love? Start by displaying sacrificial love for her and for your spouse if you've struggled with selfishness. Do you want her to grow in patience? Practice not getting upset the next time she spills her Fruit Loops or the next time she doesn't follow your directions perfectly. (I'm preaching to myself right now.)

Spiritual exercise (often referred to as the spiritual disciplines) looks different for everyone, but it will always include Scripture reading, prayer, worship, and serving others. Ask yourself if these are regular practices in your life and if your daughter is able to practice them along with you.

There is a direct correlation between your growth and hers. Trust God's Holy Spirit to enter the workout with you. The Holy Spirit is God's presence, which is with you wherever you go—even to the spiritual gym. And lean into His grace, because you will never feel perfect, just as the most disciplined athletes never believe they've arrived at perfection.

As you work, have full confidence in the God who first birthed the desire in you to grow in Him. Trust that He created that desire in your little girl too.

──────────────── LET'S PRAY ────────────────

Dear Lord,

Thank You so much for my daughter. It seems like just yesterday that she was born. And though I would love to hold onto that snapshot, You have given me constant reminders that she is growing up with each passing moment. Lord, I pray that I would look at her time in our home as a training ground for her to grow into the woman of God You have created her to be.

As she grows physically and emotionally, I pray she would also grow spiritually. May she not look at a relationship with You as an end point to be achieved, but as the beginning of a commitment and story that will develop continually from her childhood, through her teenage years, and into adulthood.

May I not look at my role as either peer and friend or taskmaster, but as a winning coach, inspiring her with my example and my constant yet humble voice of truth and grace. Lord, may my life be the primary source of her inspiration to follow You. Lord, make up for my bad decisions, laziness, and poor coaching. May Your truth soak into her soul in a way that makes Your promises sweet and nourishing. As I seek You on her behalf, make Yourself known to her in every relationship she forges, in every institution and home she steps into, and in every situation she finds herself in.

Lord, I ask that "all things work together for good" in her life as she continues to grow in You. Finish what You have started. Water what You have planted. May she become an oak of righteousness for Your glory and for the sake of the world You've made.

Father, I pray that Your Spirit would be evident in my daughter's character and that her life would demonstrate You working inside of her.

I pray that she will seek Your ways, and that as a result, her days will be full of selfless love, joy that no one can take away, peace that surpasses all understanding, and patience that overflows.

Let her kindness, goodness, faithfulness, and gentleness be evident to all. In all these things, I pray that You would teach her self-control by taking control. Let the fruit she bears be sweet and inviting to aching hearts and lost souls. Give her a yearning to know You and to seek You.

She is Yours, and I trust You with her.

Amen.

4

HER WILL

WYNTER | So you know that heart we've been talking about? The one where God has planted His Spirit and wants to grow His fruit? Yes, that one. Well, though my desire is always to grow my girls into mature young women who love the Lord with all their hearts, sometimes they move down a different path than the one I have marked out. Imagine that—a houseful of girls with individual wills, ideas, and plans! Honestly, growing up as a girl who knew what she wanted and who didn't

"The heart of man plans his way, but the LORD establishes his steps."
PROVERBS 16:9 ESV

settle for less, I expected some fight and tenacity in at least one or two of my girls. I ended up getting it in all of them in different ways. Scripture also speaks to its reality.

JONATHAN | Merriam-Webster's dictionary says the word "will" is "used to express desire, choice, willingness, consent, or in negative constructions, refusal."

God gave each of us free will, and He gave it to our girls as well. His intent was never to force us into specific actions by breaking us, but to allow us to see our own brokenness and need for Him so we would choose Him in humility.

As we shepherd our girls, our intent should be the same. Obviously, there are times as parents that we don't allow our girls a choice because it will directly threaten their health or safety or the well-being of someone else. However, as often as we can, we should be giving our girls freedom and allowing them to experience the consequences of those choices, both good and bad. Amid the consequences and experiences, they will be able to discover for themselves the value of good choices over the destructiveness of bad choices.

It should be our aim, as much as we can while still providing boundaries and protection, to allow our girls enough freedom to learn for themselves that God's way is better than their way. Our parenting should lead them down a path of understanding that the things Mommy and Daddy say are best because they line up with God's Word. We hope they learn that ultimately, He has their good in mind.

WYNTER | If we were in a crowded auditorium and I asked you to raise your hand if you have a strong-willed daughter, you might throw your entire arm into the air—perhaps as tears stream down your cheeks! On the other hand, you might sit peacefully, wondering why others are weeping in a corner!

If I rephrased my question to ask, "Do you have a daughter who challenges you in one way or another?" I suspect that even if you wouldn't describe her as strong-willed, you would say yes.

I would be the first person in the room with both hands held up high in response to either question. There are varying levels of wills in our home, and each comes with a different set of challenges! Despite the difficulties that individual wills can bring, I am grateful for the ability to see the beauty and the strength that I know exist in each of our girls. If there were a horizontal line drawn to show the ranges of agreeability in our girls, I would have tiny dots all along the spectrum.

One morning one of my girls insisted on wearing her hot-pink dress with the big orange flower in the center of the chest. She was so excited and proud of herself for picking out her own outfit. She had matched the dress with her hot-pink and white, polka dot, flowery leggings, along with her hot-pink sneakers! Her outfit was a girlie girl's dream...hot pink, flowers, and polka dots everywhere!

She came running into the room to greet me, screaming, "Look, Mommy, I'm all dressed and I match!" I looked at her and gasped! I quickly mirrored her smile and mimicked her excitement, but on the inside I wasn't so excited. I almost bit a hole in my tongue trying to hold back my real opinion!

Here's why. The dress is adorable, and so are the leggings, but together...not so much! What I failed to mention is that the bottom of her adorable hot-pink dress is brown and orange...ruffled *plaid*.

That is correct, friends. My sweet girl matched her plaid ruffled dress with her polka-dot leggings and was brimming with confidence! Her mind and her heart were set.

I thought long and hard about this one.

My first thought was, "She cannot go to school like this. It doesn't get much worse than polka dots and plaid. I am going to make her change." This was quickly followed by my second thought: "Who cares?"

Guess which thought won?

My four-year-old went off to school in orange, hot pink, brown, plaid, polka dots, and flowers. On this particular day, I decided that it just didn't matter. This wasn't a life-changing decision—it simply meant that my four-year-old went off to school...happy!

With a house full of girls, I am learning to choose my battles wisely. Sometimes I must simply let go.

I have to choose to take a stand based on what Jonathan and I value as important. Thankfully, matching patterns does not fall into that category!

On a daily or even hourly basis, our girls will make choices that we disagree with. Let's not get caught in a battle of the wills. We will not win their hearts by fighting every battle.

Here's my advice: The next time you are about to jump into the ring over an outfit, snack preference, or choice of hair bows, use these brief tips to help you decide if it's a battle worth fighting. It may be best to save your energy for another day.

- *Is it a biblical issue?* Does what your daughter wants contradict the very faith and godliness that your family professes?

- *Does it affect others?* Philippians 2:14-15 (NLT) says, "Do everything without complaining and arguing, so that no one can criticize you. Live clean, innocent lives as children of God, shining like bright lights in a world full of crooked and perverse people." Paul is reminding the believers in Philippi that Christ followers are to be like "bright lights," and we should be thinking the same thing as we send our girls out. In other words, does what our girl wants reinforce or taint her ability to shine brightly?

- *Is it in direct conflict with a family instruction or guideline?* Sometimes as a family, you will have rules that have nothing to do with right or wrong. There are some guidelines that aren't about biblical standards. For example, you may decide that your girls can't have sugar after seven p.m. on a school night. Once your standard is set, stick with it, knowing that children need to know, learn, respect, and value boundaries.

I challenge you to set the parameters and choose to focus on and fight for things that matter! Remember, to shape her will, you need to allow her the space to learn that her choices make a difference. If she never feels as though she has choice, or if she believes her decisions are always handed down from you, she will not grow in her understanding of what healthy choices look like. There is also a strong likelihood that she will resent never feeling free to make her own choices—which often leads to rebellion. Both results are ones you want to avoid as you set her up for success as a God girl and an adult.

Not all children are defined as strong-willed; however, they are all born with a will that at times can be very different from our own.

I was 24 years old when our first daughter was born. Her will has always been strong. She is also a very gifted, intelligent, and knowledgeable girl. Even in her earliest days, with a little time and very little guidance, she could figure most things out all by herself. She still can.

I am convinced that she has known how to walk and talk since day six, but she just needed to wait for her legs and mouth to catch up! And Jonathan often jokes that she was mentally ready for adulthood at age ten.

I have a very vivid memory of her being overwhelmingly frustrated as a five-month-old. There were days when she would not stop bellowing a tearless yet ferocious cry. This was not a once-in-a-while occurrence, but a habit during her earliest months. In one particular instance, her crying ebbed and flowed for a few days straight until I couldn't take it anymore. Beyond the obvious—diaper, sleep, or food—I could never fully figure out what she needed, what was wrong, or how to fix it. I eventually became worried that there was something much more serious going on. Was she sick? Was there something wrong with her belly? I now know there was nothing wrong at all.

I guess she was just welcoming me to parenthood.

As a new, young mom, I did not know what to do with her. Surely something was wrong. It had to be! So I did what I had to do. One day Jonathan and I hopped in the car and went for a two-hour drive back home to Baltimore to see my family. When we arrived, I handed my unhappy baby over to the capable hands of my aunt and immediately found an empty bed and crashed. I needed a nap! Shortly after, I awoke to the "oohs" and "ahhs" of a delightful baby girl. I was so confused and a little tearful.

I could not help but wonder, "Is it just me? Does she not like her own mother?"

My sweet aunt must have recognized the look of defeat on my face. She looked up at me and said, "This baby girl is going to be fine. There is nothing wrong with her—she just knows what she wants and can't wait to tell you what to do!" she said, quite convinced. She also burst out laughing right in my sorrow-filled face! I knew my daughter loved me, but in that moment I felt completely at a loss. Why would God give me a baby if I clearly did not know what to do with her?

At the time I did not quite know how to process what my aunt told me. I don't claim to know everything now, and at 24 I knew even less. That's a fact. So I did what I needed to do to survive, day by day.

Meaning, for months I can remember crawling out of her bedroom at night because she demanded I stand over her crib while she slept. I remember begging my mother not to "look at her" when she was calm because I didn't want to disturb her peace! I also remember holding the bottom of her foot while we repeated the drive from New Jersey to Baltimore numerous times to be with my family because I needed sleep.

My firstborn was so much work that I even prayed (okay, let me be honest) and begged God to change her personality a little—at least enough to make it easier for me to parent. Parenting her felt impossible, and I thought I was completely incapable of handling the task. I had to learn the difference between my responsibility to lead and her willingness to follow.

In those early days, I had to be satisfied with accomplishing the basics. I made sure she was fed, changed, and on a good sleeping schedule, along with the other things I knew to do by instinct and through learning. I had to do my part and trust the Lord with the rest. Thankfully, He surrounded me with others who joined me on my journey, helping me where I lacked knowledge.

I found that there was benefit to the struggle, and the things I learned in those early days have stuck with me. I've chosen to trust the same process as my daughter's will pushes against my best efforts to nurture and guide her.

Once she knew how to express herself verbally, think logically, and behave rationally (for the most part), I began trying to balance a few things. I'm still learning about the relationship between…

- Her strength as an amazing young woman, now age 13, and my authority as her mom

- Her desire for control and God's call for obedience

- Her need to express herself and my desire to fix it

I am learning how to give her the knowledge I have and the freedom she needs to process it.

Looking back, I'm so glad God did not answer my prayer. While I was busy praying for her to change so I could rest, God was graciously preparing her for His journey. As a matter of fact, when I look back at pictures and videos, I have to laugh. The determination and strength that lived inside my five-month-old's heart have grown into a passionate pursuit of God's will for her life. And that makes me smile.

There is no doubt in my mind that God is writing a beautiful story with her life as she continues to submit her will to His plan. I pray that the Lord helps me to appropriately give her the space she needs to grow in His wisdom and understanding. Thankfully, God has given me a unique opportunity to take a step back and peek into her heart and His plan.

One day while sitting on the soccer field, I received a phone call from one of my best friends, who also happens to be my cousin. Her voice was full of excitement as she briefly updated me on a recent audition she'd had for an upcoming Christian film. She skimmed over the details of the process and dove right into her main purpose for calling. "Wynter, the woman in the movie has a daughter!" she exclaimed. "Alena should audition!"

I laughed at her words and waited for her to share more about the opportunity God had given her, but she was more interested in talking about the possible opportunity for Alena. In my mind, it wasn't even a potential reality. Prior to this moment, Alena's acting career consisted of a few fireplace performances with an audience of five: my husband, me, and her three younger sisters.

But because the door was opened for her to submit a taped audition, we gave it some thought. Alena gets excited about new things, and she quickly expressed an interest in recording the few lines that were given and gave it everything she had.

As God would have it, Alena's first lines were well received, and she was immediately asked for more. Alena welcomed the challenge and rehearsed lines over and over again, working to perfect

the voice and feel of the scene. The role required a level of athleti-
cism, so one of the things she was asked for was a video showing her
athletic abilities. At one point Alena asked us to record her in the
front yard. Apparently, she was able to retain a few years of her gymnastics training, and through her strong work ethic and committed
practice, she taught herself a few new moves. We walked outside and
recorded her as we watched her execute a perfect front handspring,
something we had never seen before or encouraged.

For the first few days, we considered this opportunity little more
than a pipe dream. So after weeks of auditioning and praying, you
can only imagine the shock we all felt when she received the call. She
had gotten the part!

In the summer of 2014 she was cast in *War Room*, a movie about
the power of prayer. She played the role of Danielle Jordan—one
of the lead characters alongside Priscilla Shirer and T.C. Stallings.

Not only did this movie open as the number-one film in the
country during the weekend of its release, but it went on to become
the sixth highest-grossing Christian film of all time at the box office,
with more than $73 million in tickets sold.

Having our daughter act in *War Room* was a life-changing experience, not only for her but also for our entire family. But I don't tell
you that story to tell you about *War Room*. I tell you that story as
a larger-than-life reminder of God's plan. He uses our own will to
lead us into His purposes.

There is nothing I want more than to see my daughters live out
loud for Christ, and being a part of this film was an opportunity
for my sweet, then-ten-year-old to do just that. For eight weeks as
I watched her film, I saw Jesus at work in her life and in her heart. I
was her mom, but the film's director, Alex Kendrick, was her boss.

At times it was hard for me to watch her independence, but in
those moments I saw her work harder than I thought she could. She

demonstrated selfless love, a humbled posture, and a determined attitude.

It was wonderful. I was grateful, and I was convinced that although I play a significant role as her mother, who she is and what God has planned for her has little to do with me.

Each moment with her on set was a reminder to me that the beautiful story that is blossoming is being written by none other than the Creator Himself, God.

Since day one, I have prayed for God to grant each of my daughters a heart that yearns to know Him and a willingness to follow His lead. I have prayed fervently that He would grow them into little Jesus-chasing world changers.

But can I be honest? Answered prayers can be scary, especially when they involve my children.

Praying for our children to yearn for Christ requires selflessness and follow-through. When the Lord answers this prayer, it requires a huge amount of personal sacrifice. It demands that we totally release control and willingly sit back and watch Him work.

The longer I parent, the more evident it becomes that my children are His.

God taught me this lesson in a dramatic way when Alena was cast as Danielle. But most often God is calling us to a posture of prayer, release, and trust in the very small, seemingly insignificant moments in our lives.

And when I am speechless, unsure, or afraid of where God's plan and their submitted will to Christ will lead them, my knees hit the ground and I pray.

JONATHAN | Okay, I know what you are thinking. It's hard to relate to the story of Alena in *War Room*. It is for us as well. Remember, we have three other girls, none of whom have been in a movie.

Alena never ceased to be a normal little girl with a normal life, thank God! Most of our days look just like yours. They are filled with the everyday struggles as we lead our girls through the normal routines.

"Strong-willed" is a very broad way of describing another of our girls, Camryn, the oldest of our twins. We should have guessed how strong-willed she would be, even while Wynter was pregnant with her and her twin sister, Olivia. Even in the womb, Camryn was known as Baby A, and she is still a type A personality. She knows what she wants and will not take no for an answer. I've had more than a few run-ins with this girl, and her strength, even when she was a toddler, has kept me on my knees daily. Camryn was born with self-determination and grit that allow her to persevere through more pain and discomfort than most adults can stomach. I have yet to find a method of discipline or a process that can routinely redirect her will.

It is easy to focus our attention on potential pitfalls with her, but her strength has served her well on many occasions. I remember one time when I decided to take my girls on a collaborative daddy date. That's when I decide to take all four girls, without Mom, for a surprise date to the movies or dinner.

Needless to say, the girls were excited. We loaded into the van, arrived at the theater, bought our tickets, and ran into the lobby to get our popcorn. (I walked hurriedly, since I'm a little too proud to run into a kids' film.)

In her excitement, Camryn must have crossed feet with one of her sisters because she went face-first into the tile without bracing her fall. The hardest part of her chin caught the edge of the tile where it meets the grout and was immediately torn open. It looked gnarly and jagged and was more of a rip than a cut.

I stopped, kneeled down, and scooped her up into my arms. It was not a good scene. Within a matter of seconds our clothes were stained with blood. With all the blood and the drama of the fall, you would have expected Camryn to be in shock and hysteria. Her three sisters began freaking out immediately. They were crying, concerned for her safety and well-being. By the time some theater staff came to our aid, blood was running everywhere. To my surprise, Camryn was completely composed. She waited for directions, unfazed by what had happened. And she was the most upset by my decision to skip the movie and seek medical attention.

We quickly piled back into the car and raced to the emergency room. Wynter was out of town and couldn't pick up the other three girls, so we were all in the ER together. Thinking about it now, I guess it was still a daddy date, though a rather sad one.

Camryn sat quiet as a mouse, expressionless. She was calm, under control, and lucid. There was no rattle in her. As her sisters continued to sob, Camryn's peace was a force of fortitude. Her resolve to get through this ordeal without emotions and drama was stabilizing for me and my other three girls.

Camryn stayed this way through the entire ordeal. She sat patiently and quietly in the waiting room, even comforting her most emotional sister—her tenderhearted twin—by saying that everything was going to be all right. She endured injections of Novocain and six stitches, all while keeping perfect peace in the middle of a personal storm.

This would be the first of two similar experiences, both involving six stiches. Once in the chin, the other in her big toe. I get woozy thinking about it even now.

Although interruptions like these are not ideal, I have to say they can be gifts and opportunities. They allow us parents to take a step back from our normal view of parenting—teaching, instructing, disciplining—to witness the character that is blossoming inside our child.

In this moment, I was able to see and appreciate the beauty that God had created in my strong-willed daughters. It took my heartache over the sheer exhaustion that raising them can bring and turned it to gratitude for the power that God has placed within them. Wynter and I pray daily that this God-given gift will be a force for good and for God as our girls become leaders in their generation.

As you seek to shape your daughter's will and teach her the value of aligning her plans with God's, think about how you can be an effective tool for Him.

- *Always be the picture of a will submitted to God.* Let her see your actions and your attitude reflecting Christ. Your daughter *will* watch you in different circumstances, and you can rest assured that she *will* emulate you as you choose to emulate Christ (or not). Titus 2:7 talks about the importance of teaching those younger than us by example: "Show yourself in all respects to be a model of good works" (ESV). As you reflect Christ's goodness to her, you will be chiseling into her soul an understanding of the very grace and love of God.

- *Encourage her when her actions and attitude are Christlike and good.* Every girl needs to know that she can please her parents. When she pleases you, her heart is motivated to do it again. Sensing that she can be Christlike, she realizes He can use her—and wants to. Just as it encourages you when God smiles down on a Christlike action you take, do the same for your daughter. Of course, your affection and love are not dependent upon her actions, and she should know she is loved regardless of what she does. But to positively encourage her is a critical job that God has given you. Proverbs 22:6 tells us, "Train up a child in the way [she] should go; even when [she] is old [she] will not depart from it" (ESV). Think of it as the kind of positive affirmation a good coach gives a player who executes a winning play. It's an "Attagirl!" Your encouragement shapes her will and understanding that God is for her and so are you!

- *Discipline her appropriately when her actions and attitude are not Christlike.* Our culture is not one that supports discipline. Parents are encouraged to be their children's best friend first, but ultimately, the Bible is replete with commands that say otherwise. We are warned to bring swift and certain discipline for actions that don't reflect godly behavior. Proverbs 29:15 says, "The rod and reproof give wisdom, but a child left to himself brings shame to his mother" (ESV). There are certainly many different ways to discipline, but this verse reminds us that our girls should not be left on their own. No, we should constantly be seeking to impart wisdom to our children, and this verse reminds us that their wisdom begins with our routine, consistent, and God-honoring discipline. Your discipline is a negative consequence that teaches your daughter there are repercussions for her actions. Included in your discipline should be biblical support that reminds them of why "this is wrong" or why "this is harmful" to them or others.

"Teach me to do Your will,
For You are my God;
Let Your good Spirit lead
me on level ground."

PSALM 143:10 NASB

WYNTER | I've come to a place of gratefulness for my daughters' strength, their strong minds, and their determined hearts. I am seeing that when you raise a strong-willed, unwavering, and passionate child whose will has been cultivated to match His ways, you have a powerful woman of God!

"LORD, be gracious to us;
we long for you.
Be our strength every
morning, our salvation
in time of distress."
ISAIAH 33:2

It is our prayer that you choose to see God's perfect plan and fingerprints in your daughter's will. Her heart needs to be shaped by the Lord, and you are His primary tool for that shaping. Own that responsibility!

———————— LET'S PRAY ————————

Father,

Thank You for being an intentional God who created my daughter in a very specific way. Thank You for making, molding, and preparing her will for the plans You have ahead for her. Lord, even as You shape her, may Your Spirit lead her and protect her from the potential pitfalls that come with the strength You've given her.

And be gracious and kind to her, reminding her that her strength comes from You.

May all her strengths and the story You are writing in her life be a light for Your goodness, and may it make much of the name of Jesus.

Father, give me the wisdom, patience, and trust in You to guide her. Help me to be a craftsman's tool to help shape her without breaking her. May her brokenness come only from understanding her desperate need for You.

She is Yours, and I trust You with her.

In Jesus's name, amen.

5

HER IDENTITY

WYNTER | The familiar phrase "I have to find myself" has always made me chuckle. When I was younger, my sarcastic response was always, "Well, where exactly did you go?" I wasn't intending to be mean or insensitive, but I didn't quite understand how a person could lose the essence of their existence. The idea that a person could lose himself or herself seemed a bit bizarre—until it happened to me.

I knew my address, but I was unsure of the identity and purpose of the person residing there. I believe we all experience moments or seasons of identity misplacement or crisis. Often we associate this feeling of loss with tangible and circumstantial details such as a career choice, relationship status, or physical location. However, if we find ourselves searching for answers about our existence, what we are truly longing for is truth about our identity that can only be found in Christ.

One day I was preparing to speak to a group of teenage girls about this very topic—their identity—when I found myself face-to-face with a man amid an identity crisis. He did not know who he was. More importantly, he did not understand the truth of *whose* he was.

Tucked away in the pages of 2 Samuel, there are a few brief mentions of a man named Mephibosheth. If you read too quickly, you may miss the significant and resounding truth that lives in the details of his story—a truth that at one point or another we have all struggled to believe.

Mephibosheth had a tragic history. His father and grandfather were killed in battle. In an effort to protect him from the same enemies that had killed his father, Jonathan, and his grandfather, King Saul, Mephibosheth's nurse ran away with him. At some point on the journey, Mephibosheth was dropped and crippled for life.

Second Samuel chapter 4 tells us that Mephibosheth was royalty and the son of a prince. Yet his daily existence was not one of privilege or excitement. Instead he lived crippled, damaged, and full of fear.

Before he knew it, his circumstances began to define who he was. He set his expectations according to this new identity and consequently lived a life that was not fit for royalty.

In 2 Samuel 9, Mephibosheth shows up again. He was a little older and probably quite settled into life when, out of the blue, King David sent for him. King David was a close friend to Jonathan, Mephibosheth's father, and he wanted to give Mephibosheth the life he deserved...because of who his father was.

Second Samuel 9:8 says that Mephibosheth was clueless. He thought David considered him to be a threat to the throne because he was Saul's grandson. Fearing the worst, he bowed down and said to David, "What is your servant, that you should notice a dead dog like me?" He had no idea of his true value, though royal blood ran through his veins!

I don't know about you, but I immediately connected with this damaged man and the lie he was living. Oftentimes, I let my current circumstances, my actions, and my choices (past and present) determine my identity and how I expect to be treated.

Growing up, I found myself sorting through the many lies I'd believed. For example…

I believed I had to earn love.

I believed I was forgotten.

I believed I lacked value.

Looking back, I'm grateful that I had a family who stood firm on God's truth, constantly pushing me toward God's Word and what He had to say about who I am.

The simple truth is this: Who we *really* are has nothing to do with us.

Mephibosheth's value did not come from anything he had done—not what he looked like, not how smart he was, and not from what others said about him. His life was valuable because of who his father was. He was royalty.

This is what you must believe about yourself and what you must continue to instill in your daughter. Her value has nothing to do with where she is, what she can do, how she looks, how she dresses, or how popular she is. Her value comes from who her heavenly Father is. She needs to be reminded every day that if she is in Jesus Christ, then she is royalty!

Having four daughters, I find myself having to affirm their beauty and worth in Christ continually. The world is constantly pushing on our girls this notion that they are only valuable…

if they are thin

if they are pretty

if they are popular

if they are _____ [anything that has nothing to do with their true identity and value]

We need to be a constant voice that affirms their true identity as royal daughters of the Most High God. You see, it didn't really matter what Mephibosheth thought about himself when David called him up. He was the grandson of King Saul and the son of Jonathan—he *was* royalty. Therefore, his thoughts needed to get in line with the truth.

In the same way, as you parent your daughter, make it your aim to call out the truth of her status in Christ. Say it until she believes it. Teach it until she learns it. Impress it until she owns it! God is asking you and equipping you to be the primary voice that affirms her identity. If you don't, other voices will—but with a different message.

> "You are a chosen people, a royal priesthood, a holy nation, God's special possession, that you may declare the praises of him who called you out of darkness into his wonderful light."
>
> **1 PETER 2:9**

JONATHAN | I have to admit that identity is something I have struggled with in the past, and I continue to struggle with it to this day. But I thank the Lord for the Word of God, which reminds me of who I am as I turn its pages. I thank Him for the people He has placed around me who continue to speak truth whether I like hearing it or not. On many days, my flesh will try to tell me differently, but the Holy Spirit is always kind to remind me of the truth.

The Bible declared me royalty and sealed it with the promises of God the minute I placed my faith in Jesus Christ.

You would think that because I grew up assured of my standing in Jesus, walking in confident humility would have been natural. It was anything but.

Like many kids, I grew up worrying about what other people thought about me instead of remembering who I really was. So, though I was royalty and had responsibility in the kingdom to make life better for others, I oftentimes acted more like a peasant—worried about myself and the things I thought I needed but couldn't attain.

In high school this flaw was so great, it came with a name. It was given to me by one of my high school football coaches: One Way. Long story short, as he looked at my character, he noticed a flaw—the single-minded desire to get my own way. He wasn't impressed, and the nickname was his way of calling out the behavior. I wouldn't fully understand the significance of the name until years later. But eventually, through God's Word, the admonition of others, and the Holy Spirit, God helped me repent of that false identity and exchange it for what He called me to be—selfless.

I thank God that He changed my name and continues to remind me of that name change, even as the past tries to rear its ugly head. It took time and experience to realize that Jesus made me exactly the way He wanted, for a specific purpose and with my good in mind.

God changed the names of so many in the Bible. From Abram to Abraham and from Sarai to Sarah. From Jacob to Israel and from Simon to Peter. God's purpose for renaming His people was to signify their new identity in Him and His calling on their lives. Just like you, me, and all mankind, they struggled to remember who they were and whose they were. God's Word, the Bible, serves as a steady reminder of our true identity, and as parents we are to represent that truth to our daughters.

When one of my girls was about six years old, she was riding in the car with my wife and me. As we slowed at a light, she noticed a young man walking down the street. His pants were well below his waist, allowing his underwear to show. As we drove by, she said, "Daddy, I don't want to marry a man like that."

"What do you mean, baby?"

She replied, "Well, his pants are supposed to be over his butt."

We chuckled. But my heart beamed a little. Please know that what I'm saying has nothing to do with a judgmental attitude about how this young man wore his pants. You see, I know that one of my greatest responsibilities as a dad is teaching my daughters about what they should expect from a man. And I know this only happens two ways.

First, I get to tell them what to expect. As often as I can, I explain that a man is supposed to love God with all his heart and love others more than he loves himself. I tell them a man is supposed to be a gentleman—patient and kind and forgiving.

Second, and more importantly, my actions should teach them what to expect. I know we don't use the cliché anymore, but as a dad, my actions do speak louder than my words.

Now, please know that I never told my daughters anything about how a man is supposed to wear his pants. He could have been a very nice young man who had all the qualities I listed above. But from a long way off, my daughter noticed that this young man was not wearing his pants the way her father wore his. She noticed that there was a glaring difference, and that caused her to push back from the idea of joining in matrimony with such a distant image of manhood.

Now, though I'm open to considering a man for my girls who doesn't wear his pants just like mine, I am completely closed-minded to the idea of my daughter accepting ideas or an identity that contradicts the character of God and who He has called her to be in Him.

As a father, I will use my position in her life and my authority in our home to point her to the Word of God, day in and day out, in voice and by example. From our morning prayers to our car rides to school, from our dinnertime devotions to our evening songs, I will direct her mind, thoughts, and will toward her Creator's love letters to her. And in my daily walk, I am seeking to model Christlike behavior that stands in contrast to the lies spoken by her soul's enemy.

I'm committed to making sure that my daughters don't believe the hype and get sucked into thinking they are someone they are not. I have no doubt that the enemy has schemes to create short-term and long-term memory loss about who they are and whose they are. He wants to use everything around them and is looking for a hook, and those hooks can be very specific in the life of a little girl.

"Do you not know that your bodies are temples of the Holy Spirit, who is in you, whom you have received from God? You are not your own; you were bought at a price. Therefore honor God with your bodies."

1 CORINTHIANS 6:19-20

He wants to use body image.

He wants to use her relationships.

He wants to use her sexuality.

He wants to use her doubts, fears, and insecurities.

Let's talk about our daughters' bodies for a moment, as it's often the place where the enemy tries to weave a web of lies. Let's talk about the truth.

First Corinthians 6:19-20 is God's message to you and to your daughter. Its author, the apostle Paul, was speaking to the church at Corinth in Greece specifically about sexual purity. It's obvious that many in this church were struggling with the purpose of their bodies, and Paul wrote them in an attempt to straighten them out. And we're thankful he did, because his voice and God's Word on this topic are still as true today as they were back then.

It is important to remember that your daughter's body is a little sanctuary.

Paul started with a simple truth. He told the Corinthians that their "bodies are temples of the Holy Spirit." In plain language, he was telling them that their bodies housed the very presence of God in the person of the Holy Spirit. He uses the word "temple" (or "sanctuary"), a reference to the Old Testament and the place where God's Spirit dwelled. In saying this, Paul was referring to the Corinthian believers' worth.

You see, God's Spirit didn't rest just anywhere. The sanctuary was a place of purity and cleanliness. It was written in the Law and carried out in custom that not just anyone could go into the sanctuary, but only the priest. And even he could only go in once a year, and only after having gone through ceremonial rituals to make sure he was ready. You can read more about the sanctuary in Exodus 26 and Leviticus 16, but for now, just remember that God's Spirit inhabited this special place in a special way—a place set apart for His glory.

And that is where we start with our little girls. Even in their earliest days, we should be teaching them that God created them and their bodies to be a place where He could live. We should be shaping their minds with the truth that they are set apart—a temple, if you will—a place where God's glory and awesomeness can dwell day in and day out. Because of your voice in their lives and your constant reminder to them of who they are in Christ, there should be no doubt in their minds that they have intrinsic, irreplaceable worth. They should have a sense of dignity that comes only from knowing who they are in Jesus.

The world and many outside influences will do their best to attach your daughter's value to how skinny she is, how pretty she is, or how curly or how straight her hair is, depending on your culture. The television will tell her that she needs a boyfriend and that her worth is tied to how someone else views her. Myriad stories are being sold these days to girls who aren't being shaped by truth.

But your goal, my goal, and a big part of our purpose as parents is to inundate them with a different message on an overwhelming basis. We must remind them that God desires not only to be *with* them, but to be *in* them. And that if they have trusted Christ for the forgiveness of their sins and eternal life, then His very real and awesome presence is living inside of them in the person of the Holy Spirit. Their body is His house, and as such it is a holy place—a dwelling, set aside for them to meet with Him.

And just as God's sanctuary was built to serve a greater purpose than any other house in Israel, our bodies are built to serve a greater purpose as well. Our daughter's body has purpose.

God's presence with His people Israel was in part to make them "a light for the nations" (Isaiah 49:6 ESV). Israel was to be His servant, bringing God's salvation to those in need. Just as the people of Israel were clearly God's servants, Paul reminded the Corinthians, "You are not your own; you were bought at a price." Paul is reminding them (and you and me) that we were purchased—redeemed—through Jesus's death and resurrection. He is affirming that they were taken from darkness and brought into light so they could shine the light of Jesus on those they met. In fact, the author of Acts, another book in the New Testament, quotes Isaiah 49:6 from the Old Testament, talking about Christ followers: "I have made you a light for the Gentiles, that you may bring salvation to the ends of the earth" (13:47).

Now, I know that can sound like an intimidating task for you and me to own, much less teach to our girls. But in this verse Paul was talking much less about what they were supposed to do and more about who they were.

As Christ followers, we are already His!

We are trusting that the light of Jesus is already shining in and through us. And we are affirming, reminding, and retelling our daughters who they already are in Christ! They are the light of the world. They are His servants.

As the ultimate truth tellers in their life, it is our responsibility to be the loudest voice about their bodily position. We should be a stronger voice than culture or any other outside influencer—reminding them that their body belongs to Christ, and it's in their service to Him that they will find their ultimate purpose and satisfaction.

"I urge you, brothers and sisters, in view of God's mercy, to offer your bodies as a living sacrifice, holy and pleasing to God—this is your true and proper worship."

ROMANS 12:1

We must relentlessly remind our girls that they are valuable temples where God's Spirit rests. They have been given life and an earthly body to serve God's purposes, and any influence that tries to persuade them otherwise is a voice contrary to God's Word. Those false influences should not make it past the spiritual boundaries you have hardwired into them through time in God's Word and time spent with you. Our goal is to silence the voice of the enemy in their lives that would suggest that they've been created for any other purpose.

The very last part of 1 Corinthians 6:20 says, "Therefore honor God with your bodies." Paul is encouraging us that our mission as Christ followers is to live in such a way that God's character is displayed through our bodies, in our very identity.

Your life should be that very display for your daughter. In you, with God's grace, she should see the very character of God and what it looks like for God to be seen in your body. Your voice should be the strongest clarion call.

From the way she dresses, to the way she responds to authority, to how she feels about herself, may it be that God uses your life and your voice to mold, protect, and keep your daughter's body for His Spirit to be at home.

With every opportunity I have, I am pouring the truth of who my girls really are into them whether they realize the need for it or not.

I'm committed to making sure that my girls know the truth even before they feel it. That they understand even before they are convinced. And that they can spot a lie from a long way off.

I'm committed to seeking the Holy Spirit for myself and begging Him to guide each of my daughters. After all, my ability and willpower can only go so far. I am dependent on the Holy Spirit's power to redeem her, to summon her, and to call her by His name.

Just as David summoned Mephibosheth and showed him who he was in the kingdom of Israel, I pray that our Lord summons each of our girls and reminds them of who they are in the kingdom of God.

WYNTER | Here are a few verses that are worth repeating to our daughters daily about their identity, regardless of whether they are asking these questions yet.

- *Am I special?* "I will give thanks to You, for I am fearfully and wonderfully made; wonderful are Your works, and my soul knows it very well" (Psalm 139:14 NASB).

- *Am I pretty?* "God created man in His own image, in the image of

"But now, this is what the Lord says—he who created you, Jacob, he who formed you, Israel: 'Do not fear, for I have redeemed you; I have summoned you by name; you are mine.'"
ISAIAH 43:1

God He created him; male and female He created them"
(GENESIS 1:27 NASB).

- *Is it okay that I am different?* "Now there are varieties
  of gifts, but the same Spirit…One and the same Spirit
  works all these things, distributing to each one individu-
  ally just as He wills" (1 CORINTHIANS 12:4,11 NASB).

- *Am I enough?* "He saved us, not on the basis of deeds
  which we have done in righteousness, but according to
  His mercy, by the washing of regeneration and renewing
  by the Holy Spirit" (TITUS 3:5 NASB).

"We have stopped evaluating others from a human point of view.
At one time we thought of Christ merely from a human point of view.
How differently we know him now! This means that anyone who
belongs to Christ has become a new person. The old life is gone;
a new life has begun!

And all of this is a gift from God, who brought us back to himself
through Christ. And God has given us this task of reconciling people
to him. For God was in Christ, reconciling the world to himself,
no longer counting people's sins against them. And he gave us this
wonderful message of reconciliation. So we are Christ's ambassadors;
God is making his appeal through us."

2 CORINTHIANS 2:16-20 NLT

---------------------------- LET'S PRAY ----------------------------

Heavenly Father,

Thank You for Your Word and its constant reminder of who I am in You. Thank You for seeing past my flaws and issues, and thank You for changing my name and making me royalty in Your kingdom. Give me confidence in my true identity.

As I continue to grow into who You have called me to be, may You help me in calling out who my daughter is in You. Lord, give me insight and wisdom to see the lies that the enemy might be attempting to sow into her life, and point me to Your Word, which speaks the truth of who she really is.

May my voice and may my life speak more loudly than the salacious lies of the enemy. May she see my confidence in You and desire to mirror it. May Your voice and may Your Word speak through me and through others, reminding her of her status as royalty in Your kingdom.

She is Yours, and I trust You with her.

In Jesus's name, amen.

6

HER OBEDIENCE

JONATHAN | "Obedience." It's a word that often makes me cringe. It brings to mind the last time one of my daughters was disobedient and I felt like an utter failure as a parent. "Failure" is another word that makes me cringe because it reminds me of the many ways I've felt like a failure in my desire to create an obedient spirit in each of my girls. Try as I may—and believe me, I try continually—creating an obedient spirit in my daughters has been one area where I have often felt overwhelmed and underprepared. If you asked me which of the topics in this book I pray the most about, this would be it.

I ask God often to put an obedient spirit in each of my girls because I know they will find their greatest joy in obedience.

Ephesians 6:1-3 is probably the first verse I memorized as a child. Frankly, it's

"Children, obey your parents in the Lord, for this is right. 'Honor your father and mother'— which is the first commandment with a promise—'so that it may go well with you and that you may enjoy long life on the earth.'"

EPHESIANS 6:1-3

the verse I wrote more times on white lined paper than any other, as my parents were seeking to shape a heart of obedience in me. They knew the importance of impressing God's Word upon my heart—not because I appreciated it at the time, but because they knew I would eventually absorb and grasp its value.

And so I wrote…and wrote…and wrote. With each inscription, my mind was more and more saturated with the reality of the Scripture's truth. Without my knowing it, the message was going deeper and deeper past the cognitive level—and only later would I come to fully understand, appreciate, and honor the command given in these verses. Eventually, I would be convicted of the fact that my parents had my best interests at heart—joy and a long, satisfying life—as did the Lord in giving me the command!

Similarly, Wynter and I have sought to impress the truth of Paul's words onto the hearts of our girls. On most days it seems as if it goes in one ear and out the other, but we pray and hold on to God's promise that He will be faithful to complete what we cannot.

WYNTER | We have some really good stories of our efforts to instill obedience in our girls, and I thought I'd share a fun, light, and humorous example—the bedtime blues. Every parent of small children has experienced them. It's when bedtime finally arrives and you tuck your kids into bed and pray that they stay. However, they continually reappear to ask for water, a new pillow, or a Band-Aid.

I could write an entire blues record recapping our bedtime adventures! I like to use this example because it illustrates some of the frustrations I've had. Yes, the challenges have changed and sometimes seem more complicated, but what we are seeking—an obedient heart—has not.

A while ago a friend told me about a book she and her husband were reading that offered help with the bedtime blues. What

I gathered from her synopsis was summed up in this one directive to your children:

"It is bedtime, and I don't want to see you or hear you."

If you saw them or heard them, there was one consequence: *work!*

She and her husband gave it a go. She explained that after a short run of emptying the trash cans, one of her girls got the point and headed to bed. The younger one opted to sweep the back porch, but the thrill of sweeping in the dark only lasted a few minutes before she headed off to bed as well!

There were no tears (from her, her husband, or her kids), and there were no discussions. It seemed as though they had creatively shown their kids that life is about their actions and subsequent consequences. They were well on their way toward convincing their girls of the joy found in obedience. Sounds simple and perfect, right? I was inspired!

I mentioned it to Jonathan, and we were all set. We were actually a little excited about bedtime and anticipated presenting the new trick we had up our sleeves!

We put the girls to bed as normal but with the added phrase, "Mommy and Daddy do not want to see you, and we do not want to hear you."

There was silence for about ten minutes, and then the games began. We could hear Camryn and Olivia in their room playing as if it were two in the afternoon!

Following my friend's instructions, we went up and told them to come downstairs. Their facial expressions were a mix of confusion and a hint of anticipation as they followed us down.

This was going to be good. (Or so we thought.)

Kaitlyn heard what was happening and insisted on being a part. (I should have known something would go wrong.)

I explained to each girl that Mommy and Daddy stay up to get work done, and if they were going to be awake, then they needed to get some work done too.

I promise I saw smirks on two of their three little faces, which was another clue I missed. In that moment, I should have known we were in for a long evening!

I sent one of my girls to the laundry room to sort through a mountain of shoes in the milk crates. With four girls, two feet per girl, and an embarrassing number of shoes, she had her work cut out for her.

I sent another one to the game closet with instructions to organize, clean out, and sort through every puzzle and board game. Nothing seems fun about that, right?

Then we told my third girl to get the broom. The kitchen and bathrooms were all hers!

Jonathan caught my eye and whispered, "Uh-oh…they look thrilled!"

Feeling confident that the method that worked for my friend would work for us, I nodded back and said, "Just wait."

Wait is just what we did. After an hour and ten minutes of pleasant cleaning, I had a clean laundry room, an organized game closet, clean floors, a headache…and three little girls asking for more!

I honestly could not think of another thing for them to do in the house, so I sent them out back to our deck. It's dark in the evening because our deck is covered by a canopy of tree limbs and foliage, so it's a bit scary even for me. You should also know that a family of raccoons frequented that deck and most likely lived somewhere below it in the creek or possibly even underneath! Don't judge me. I was desperate for obedience and willing to try any proven methods to reach this end.

I had followed my friend's instructions exactly, and here my kids were asking for more. I guess I can say we had some success, because we taught our children a level of cleanliness, but it wasn't what we were hoping for!

The next morning, I ordered the book. Clearly I needed to read it for myself.

I wish I could say Jonathan and I have found a perfect method for encouraging obedience, but sadly, I can't. No, we still find ourselves excited over small wins but discouraged when one of our girls displays outright defiance. So we continue to work at it and to pray to God about it.

JONATHAN | Convincing our girls to clean their rooms, to pick up their toys strewn across the backyard, and to joyfully follow our commands can be stressful. And encouraging them to spend real time with the Lord by way of a devotional or quiet time in prayer before they turn on the television or pursue their weekend activities can seem impossible and physically exhausting. The particular circumstances can vary from day to day, but stirring their hearts and spirits toward obedience is rarely easy. It can be a true party killer on a peaceful Saturday morning at home, to say the least. But we've come to grips with the fact that at some level, this is just part of the parenting journey.

Like our parents before us, we choose to dig in. We choose to take them to Scripture. And we choose to pray. But we don't stop there. One of the beautiful things about parenting is that it truly is a journey. With each waking morning there are new graces and new opportunities—both for you and for your daughter. We tend to look at each day as its own clinical trial. We can test new methods, tweak, and update, but there are a few practical mainstays for us and for you.

Utilize Positive Reinforcement

For one of my daughters, it could be the reward at the end of a task. It's seeing the prize at the end of the race. It could be as simple as a stick of gum or as complicated as an elaborate outing that they concocted—froyo and a trip to see the latest girlie movie about singing, frogs, fish, or princesses. We do not encourage bribery, but utilizing incentives in training can prove effective. What better way to teach your daughter that there is joy in obedience than finding new and fun ways to reward behavior that honors God and her parents.

Discourage Through Negative Consequences

Another daughter could be more motivated by a desire to avoid punishment. She may not want to deal with the consequences that result from disobedience. I should mention that this style of motivation has zero effect on one of my daughters. Her ability to withstand isolation and loss far exceeds my ability to impose any of these consequences—hence our use of positive reinforcements with her. Her will can be so strong that the agony of enduring any negative reinforcement pales in comparison to the embarrassment and humility that comes with submission.

Now, that doesn't mean I don't follow through with the negative consequences. You just have to. I say to my girls often, "Was it worth it?" I may add, "You get to pick your actions, but you can't choose the consequences." It's just my simple reminder that consequences are a normal part of every action, for good or for bad.

My wife's uncle has a doctorate in sociology, and he once told me that for this method to prove successful, the discipline must be swift, severe, and certain. I've tried to take his advice, and at times I've done this well, but at other times I've completely bombed. It probably has to do with the combination of my occasional impatience in following through on the discipline itself and my own tender heart toward my girls. It's a delicate balance, with loving firmness on one end and gracious patience on the other. Some parents balance it better than others, but if you want to see it the most clearly demonstrated, just look at the Israelites on their journey from Egypt to the Promised Land. The Lord's dance with His people from discipline to grace over and over again is nothing short of perfectly executed fathering.

But enough on methods of motivating and more on what we are really after in all this—humble hearts that seek to honor the Lord.

"The desire of the humble You have heard, O LORD; You make their heart attentive."

PSALM 10:17 MEV

Always Look to Affirm

It's one thing for me to tell my daughters to say "please," or for me to hound them to push in their chairs after breakfast and clear their spot at the table, but it's a wholly different thing for them to get to this place without having to be asked. When I see this good behavior in my kids, I try to call it out! I quickly seek to encourage them in that moment, to affirm that they are on the right track with a big, hearty hug or a "great job" and an "I'm so proud of you!"

Recognize When You See Growth

I'll never forget coming home from one quick, exhausting business trip. Through the family room window, my girls saw my car pull into the carport behind our home and quickly scurried around to our patio to welcome me into the house. I could barely put my bags down before their 16 arms and legs began to drag me to the family room and bring me into their world. I assumed they were playing a board game or were in need of a daddy or a police officer for a make-believe world they had created.

As I walked into the living room, loud worship music was playing.

There was a stool in the front of the room with chairs and couches lined up facing the stool. Kaitlyn took her position on the stool and began making announcements. Alena, Camryn, and Olivia quickly sat in the line of chairs, and I immediately recognized them as congregants. Before taking their seats, they threw me down in the front row. I walked into the house that evening tired and exhausted, but within 60 seconds my heart was warm and my eyes were glowing as I realized my girls were worshipping God and "playing church." Moments later the announcements ended, and Kaitlyn introduced the worship team—her three sisters. They switched the music and began a worship chorus with hands raised and hearts passionate toward the Lord.

In that moment, I discovered my girls doing instinctively what I had often tried to motivate them to do every day—invite God into their day. I couldn't have been a happier father because I clearly saw a motivation and a heart for the Lord in all my girls.

Of course, I see this in other ways that have little to do with "playing church." I see it when one of them sacrifices a second piece of candy they were given to share with their sister who has none. I see it when my oldest sacrifices her alone time to help her little sister with a math sheet. I see it when I watch one of my girls follow my direction with intentionality and swiftness. If you take the time to notice, you will see in your young daughter a desperate hope and desire to obey. Look for it. Search for it in every situation and call it out!

Remind your daughters that in all these things, they are worshipping God. They need to know that their obedient service is worship to our Lord—just as much as any singing or church service ever will be.

Romans 12:1 is a constant reminder of this reality to you and to your daughters. It says, "I urge you therefore, brothers, by the mercies of God, that you present your bodies as a living sacrifice, holy and acceptable to God, which is your reasonable service of worship" (MEV). Use this truth to remind them that whenever they serve others, they are serving God and worshipping Him. When you celebrate this in them, they will resonate with this Scripture. As they view your celebration, they will be further drawn in to the joy of obedience, the joy of worship, and the joy of serving others and God. Those are all wrapped into one!

It starts with the basics. It can seem nearly impossible to coach, teach, and train, but we continue all three. Even amid distractions at our dinnertime devotions, I need to press through. But I need to do it with patience and grace. When my girls decide on Saturday morning that they aren't motivated to clean the living room, do I just say, "That's okay, girls, I'll do it"? Or do I threaten them with angry warnings of coming wrath? Heaven forbid! No, I join them in the mess, displaying an attitude of self-control, leaning on the Holy Spirit, remembering that Jesus Himself joined me in my mess. He has given me opportunity after opportunity to find joy in obedience.

The most important tactic to employ as you attempt to coach, teach, and train your daughter—leading her into obedience—is not a skill that you learn or a process that you implement. It's actually much more basic than that. You see, you can teach for hours on end, and you can train for months and even years, but if you aren't cultivating an intimate relationship with your daughter, then your efforts will probably be fruitless.

Think about your relationship with God. I don't know your story, but I would go out on a limb and guess that it isn't the severity of God—His Law or His judgment—that motivates you to follow Him through a relationship with Jesus. It was His goodness, His mercy—His loving-kindness—that drew you toward His way. It was realizing all that He has done for you, having laid everything down so that you might have opportunity after opportunity, day after day, to grow further into His will. Romans 2:4 (NASB) explains that it is "the kindness of God [that] leads you to repentance."

Likewise, as we imitate our heavenly Father in His patience, we draw our daughters into an experience of grace that is convincing. As we practice restraint, even from rightful judgment and discipline, we grant space for them to make conscious, mindful decisions toward obedience. And as we display the kindness of Christ Himself, they see in us the very nature of God that turns hearts and minds toward righteousness.

As we do all that we can to cultivate hearts of obedience in our girls, may we never forget that the love God showed us, which we need daily, is the same love they need each and every day. May we remember that one of their primary views of God will be expressed through how we parent. May we consider their tender hearts and may we never "exasperate" our girls, but instead "bring them up in the training and instruction of the Lord" (Ephesians 6:4)—with full measures of the grace, restraint, and kindness offered to us in our relationship with Christ Jesus.

─────────────── LET'S PRAY ───────────────

Father,

Thank You so much for dealing so graciously with me over the years. Time and time again, I have looked at Your call for obedience in my own life with disdain and resentment, thinking that it was a roadblock to my joy. But You have been patient with me, gently reminding me that my greatest joy is found in following Your commands and living a life that honors You.

As I seek to train obedience in my own daughter, may I take the same perspective that You took with me. Instead of turning a blind eye to disobedience as one extreme or ruling with an iron fist as the other, help me to join my daughter, right in the middle of her mess. With every method of training and discipline I attempt, whether it be positive, negative, or a little bit of both, may my daughter see my attempts as those of a loving parent who is seeking her greater joy. When she does choose obedience, help me to see it and appreciate it. When she doesn't, help me to trust Your Word and follow through on Your call on my life as the lead voice for obedience in her life.

Lord, help me to do my part. Help me to own this role, while leaving the results to You.

She is Yours, and I trust You with her.

Amen.

HER RELATIONSHIP WITH
GOD—FINAL THOUGHTS

M any distractions, both good and bad, vie for parents' attention. One day a flood of girls' activities seemed to land on
our doorstep with an overwhelming sense of responsibility and
urgency. "Mommy and me" activities were easy enough to manage.
But before we knew it, we had gymnastics, soccer, dance, basketball,
track, voice lessons, youth group, student government, and chess
club. These are all good things—don't get me wrong. But the pressure to invest so significantly in these areas comes from the world,
not from the Lord. As a family, we had to take inventory of our
investments and make a conscious decision to shift our time from
temporal things to the eternal. We had to prioritize the things that
really mattered, starting with their relationship with God.

Your daughter's relationship with God is more important than
any other, and it shapes the rest of the relationships she will have in
her life, starting with you and your nuclear family and fanning out
to the world.

Think About It

1. Are you establishing the importance of knowing God in your home (versus knowing *about* God)? In what ways are you encouraging your girls to get to know God personally for themselves?

2. How is your life serving as an example for your daughter to own her growth in Christ?

3. In what ways do you see the Lord using your daughter's will to further His purposes? How has He used yours?

4. Does your daughter connect her desires and dreams to God's ultimate plan for her life? How can you continue to encourage this in her?

5. Have you tied your discipline and quest for obedience in your home to joy? If not, how can you?

PART 2

HER
RELATIONSHIP
WITH YOU

HER RELATIONSHIP WITH YOU—LET'S GET STARTED

The weight and responsibility of being a parent can often seem like too much to tackle, especially as you ride the emotional roller coaster with your girl. If you don't take a step back to enjoy life with her, you can quickly get lost in a world of expectations and obligations—losing the happiness that rests in the journey of raising her.

Moving forward, let's discuss the time we spend with our treasures! Whether we are taking time to enjoy a spontaneous dance party, to join them in a jump on the trampoline, to snuggle with them and a book in your favorite chair, or to team up and build a sand castle, devoting these moments of retreat are what help us refocus our efforts and our purpose. It is

"Children are a gift from the LORD; they are a reward from him."

PSALM 127:3 NLT

an important but enjoyable challenge to align our efforts with God's plan. Seeing our girls smile, listening to them laugh, and viewing life through their lens is what fuels true joy.

Additionally, building our relationship with our girls is the most effective way to grow and maintain our voice in their lives. Have you ever heard the saying, "Rules without relationship lead to rebellion"? Well, this is true of our relationship with God, and it's a warning for us as parents in our relationship with our daughters as well.

We have the best intentions, no doubt, but even our best efforts can get in the way of true, authentic, and meaningful relationship. Let's start by talking about that very thing.

7

YOUR EFFORT

JONATHAN | I have this vision in my head of being a father who wakes up each morning feeling the fullness of the life that I have in Jesus Christ. In this vision, I have an unshakable confidence in who I am in God. A John the Baptist of sorts. I get out of bed feeling fully forgiven, fully loved, and fully capable of handling the task He has placed in front of me. I have forgotten yesterday's mistakes as if they never happened, and I'm ready to attack the day with ferociousness and the confidence that everything I do has purpose and that God is using me in every moment.

But these days, and especially as I write, that vision is hard to maintain. That confidence I felt when I awoke this morning now evades me. And though I know the truth of what God tells me about His forgiveness and love for me and the confidence I can have in both, if I'm honest with myself, I often see my faults and my failures in a much more prominent way. Especially when I am parenting.

Throughout the day I am reminded that I'm not a perfect father. I struggle with a hormonal teenage daughter to whom I can't say the right things. She seems discouraged many days, which I know is normal for girls in this stage, but for some reason I feel powerless to invade her space with the love and joy that she desperately needs.

More times than not I spend my time doling out commands—"pick up your shoes" and "straighten up your room"— when I should be expressing my loving-kindness and the gentle prodding that a good father should exude as he imitates his gentle and kind God.

"Thanks be to God! He gives us the victory through our Lord Jesus Christ."

1 CORINTHIANS 15:57

I wish I could say these scenarios aren't a normal, nagging part of my life, but they are. As I rest each night, I wrestle with my imperfection and how my efforts often fall short of what God expects of me as a father.

On my great days, I realize that my best efforts with my girls are average. I'm not into comparing myself with others, but I can't help but see some of the quality dads around me who seem to be perfectly patient and forever fun-loving with their girls. They always seem to be in a perfect mood, and when I run into them, they can quickly make my great day feel average.

But it's with these very real and honest emotions that I'm driven to seek the Lord. In light of my shortcomings, I know I am in desperate need of His intervention in parenting my girls. I have to go back to the Word of God.

Maybe my honesty makes you cringe, but I believe that our greatest achievements in life start with humble self-reflection and acceptance of who we are on our own. I believe that we must see our efforts for what they really are—well-intentioned at times but imperfect at best. Yes, when comparing our efforts to another parent's, we might feel better about ourselves, but ultimately what our girls need from us is greater than what we have to give. And that is why we need nothing short of a Christ-infused parenting life that comes only by way of relationship with Christ. Our relationship with Him instills confidence in His power. One of the greatest things about being a follower of Jesus is that you know there is always grace at the end of the day and new mercies in the morning.

I am committed to preparing the way for the Lord's work in my girls' lives, but my efforts are often flawed. There is no getting around it. So I stand guilty, ready to take my efforts to the Lord, humbly willing to seek Him to help me do what I can't and seeking His favor to make up the difference.

WYNTER | In my early years of mothering four girls, tasks like running to the grocery store seemed impossible. I normally didn't do it. I would carefully plan my outings around a time when Jonathan or another compassionate soul would be available to temporarily relieve me of my maternal duties. But I recall one day when I felt particularly brave and planned a trip to the store with all four girls.

I really thought I could handle it. I'm not sure what I actually thought I was going to buy or where I would put it, considering my cart was full before I even walked through the doors!

I can only imagine how I must have looked. A five-year-old tugging at my left thigh. A three-year-old waddling on my right. And a shopping cart loaded with two infant car seats.

I was *that* mom. The mom you watch in awe and amazement—and a twinge of pity.

We were strolling the aisles pretty seamlessly when somewhere between the cereal and toothbrushes it happened. The moment all parents dread...

"I have to go potty!"

I thought to myself, "Oh no!"

I tried to ignore her three cries, but as I watched her hand cup her bottom, I knew I was in trouble.

We scurried through the aisles back to the front of the store and reached the entrance to the restroom, greeted by a sign that read, "No shopping carts allowed beyond this point."

Panicking, I began to play out two scenarios in my head:

Scenario one: Remove my two infant seats and carry my twins one by one into the restroom, while towing along the two older girls. Sit the seats on the floor outside the stall, line the paper and load the three-year-old, wash hands, and head back out to the cart.

Scenario two: Leave my cart, my twins, and my five-year-old outside the restroom. Within seconds, I knew that I only had one actual option!

I took a final scan of the store. I guess I thought one final look before I began the process might give me some new insight, but there was nothing.

Finally, in complete desperation, I whispered a simple prayer, "Lord, help me!" In that moment, out of nowhere, I saw a familiar face strolling toward me. I practically threw my cart in her direction as I yelled, "I'll explain when I get back!"

"Seek first the kingdom of God and His righteousness, and all these things will be provided for you."

MATTHEW 6:33 HCSB

I'm not sure I've recovered from this experience. However, it has surely served its purpose. I often recall this experience to remind myself that *God sees me and hears my prayers.*

He is our source when we feel alone and unprepared, and even when we are facing seemingly impossible situations. He has provided all that is needed for the task at hand.

JONATHAN | I want to encourage you with two things. First, you are enough. You are enough for God to use, and He has chosen and prepared you specifically for this journey. He knows your gifts and your talents. He knows your shortcomings and your struggles.

"For just as the heavens are higher than the earth, so [God's] ways are higher than your ways and [God's] thoughts higher than your thoughts."

ISAIAH 55:9 NLT

Second, God uses your "enough" when you acknowledge you're "not enough" without a close and intimate walk with Jesus.

Here are three things to encourage you as you think about your efforts:

- *Your effort is simply an effort.* Does your effort matter? Of course it does! But you can relax knowing that God is in control and has given you all that you need, including Himself!

- *God's promises are true, regardless of your shortcomings.* You don't need to be perfect. Lean heavily on the Lord's promises when you are confronted with your shortcomings.

- *The best thing you can do is pray.* As much as we want to, we parents will never be the only source of our children's growth and maturity. I'm sure you can attest to the fact that the Lord used many people, places, and things (good and bad) in your life to draw you closer to Himself. Prayer matters, and God will use it to grow your trust in Him and shape your daughter into the follower of Christ that He has called her to become.

God has given you the gift of your daughter on purpose. As unprepared or as prepared as you may feel right now, know that God has called you to this journey.

God sees you. He knows you. And He is with you.

She is His, and so are you.

──────────────── LET'S PRAY ────────────────

Lord Jesus,

I am simply overwhelmed as I consider what's ahead of me—the task of training and preparing my daughter for life. I know I do not have what it takes.

I know that You are my source, and I pray that You would help me to rely on You for wisdom and guidance.

I pray that You would bless my effort and be gracious in my failure.

Bring godly mentors, friends, and tools into my life to assist me in my weaknesses, and may Your Spirit and grace be the key to opening her heart.

I accept the full responsibility that You have put on me, but I relinquish all control to You.

As much as I have planned, it never seems that my plans match up with Yours. And though sometimes I've been disappointed that things haven't worked out the way I want, I thank You that Your thoughts and Your plans trump mine. I thank You that You are working things together for good because I love You, and I ask that You would continue to extend Your grace and love to me as I stumble down the road on this journey of parenting my daughter.

She is Yours, and I trust You with her.

Amen.

8

YOUR PRESENCE

JONATHAN | When my girls first dropped into this world, I didn't know what to expect. My relationship with them was limited to all five pounds one ounce, five pounds two ounces, six pounds eleven ounces, and seven pounds five ounces of their tiny, droopy frames. Feed them, hold them, bathe them, comfort them, and my most favorite of all, change their diapers. (Joking!) I wasn't welling up with feelings of affection for my girls at that point, and my time spent with them didn't strike me as all that endearing during the first few weeks of their lives—but boy was it intimate! Nothing says intimacy like a blowout diaper that gets under your fingernails. And nothing invades your space more than a restless night of rocking a baby girl who can't seem to stay asleep for more than two hours.

Not long into learning this "new dad" routine, I began to feel thankful for my daughters and the opportunity to care for them in very physical and tangible ways. I can honestly say that my dependent, helpless infant girls gave me a new understanding of how God cares for you and me, especially when we are unable to care for ourselves. I began to see how a loving God could continue to clean us up when all we do is keep creating messes for Him. I began to see how He can envision lives for us that are much larger than where we are in our spiritual infancy. And I started to trust Him a bit more to provide the resources necessary for my nutrition, rest, comfort, and spiritual health.

I'm thankful for qualities in God that I have glimpsed during the earliest days with my girls. And I'm thankful to be able to provide that same type of care, mimicking God's character and care for me physically.

My girls weren't fully aware of what I was doing for them, and I really wasn't cognizant of much at that point in my life either. It was a day-to-day grind, and sleepless nights kept my brain in a continual fog for about five years. But despite the grind, my presence changed everything for my girls. It mattered then, and it matters now.

WYNTER | In those early days, intimacy with my daughters came easily. As a new mom with my new babies, I felt an instant connection. In addition to the physical intimacy that Jonathan mentioned above, I had an emotional intimacy that ran deep as I nurtured their tiny bodies.

However, as the girls' physical dependency lessened, it became easier to withdraw, and I found myself having to choose to stay close.

Our dinner table is one of the most beautifully chaotic places in our home. It is where memories are made, no doubt. It can be noisy, intense, messy, and loud. Yet at the same time it is full of joy and laughter. Sometimes I remember to capture its beauty, and sometimes I am overwhelmed by its chaos.

On one occasion I experienced the latter. Here is what happened.

Immediately after the last plate was cleared from our dinner table, I quickly escaped, hoping no one would notice. Nothing was wrong; it had just been one of those days. Rather, one of those weeks. I am sure you get the idea. I just needed a moment of silence.

I wanted to be alone, and I didn't want anyone to notice. Everyone else was so happy, and for no particular reason I just wasn't. I knew it was my own problem, and I did not want to put a damper on their mood. From my point of view, I was doing everyone a favor by removing my presence. So without saying a word, I simply got up, walked down the hall, and slipped into my bedroom. I didn't close the door behind me because I wanted to avoid any sounds that may have announced my departure. I found a corner in my bedroom and sat quietly.

Looking back, I realize I was being a bit dramatic, but I am pretty sure you've been there too!

After a few moments of sitting there, I heard footsteps creeping down the hall. I listened as those little feet approached my door, and I caught a quick glimpse of their owner as she peeked in and turned away quickly. It was Olivia, our baby, the youngest of our twins. She is tenderhearted and inquisitive. I figured she needed something, so I called her back and braced myself.

I assumed she would say, "Can you help me with…?" or "Where is my…?" But she didn't. She walked back in my room, and with her breath hitting my cheeks she whispered, "What are you doing, Mommy?"

"Nothing," I replied. "What do you need?"

Her next few words destroyed me—for the better.

She just looked me in the eyes and said, "Nothing. I just like to be around you."

Having no idea of the imprint she had just made on my heart, she shrugged her shoulders and galloped back down the hall. I remained in my quiet place, buried my face in my pillow, and cried happy tears.

In that moment I remembered something I had forgotten along the way. I had forgotten that my actual presence matters. Honestly, I am not sure I ever truly realized it did prior to this moment. Sure, as a mother, I knew I was needed. I knew I played a crucial role in my daughter's development and well-being, but somewhere underneath the folded laundry, signed permission slips, and gallon-sized plastic bags of leftovers, I lost sight of a major truth. In my home, even amid the chaos and the mess, I am not only needed but also wanted.

My daughters and yours do not simply need us around to take care of them. They long to laugh at our jokes, listen to the stories that make us just like them, and see our smiles sitting across from them.

Parenting is about so much more than being needed. Yes, we are needed for many things, but our presence is actually longed for and desired by our daughters.

If you are like me and find yourself in a moment of withdrawal, remember this: They like being around you.

JONATHAN | Unlike Wynter, I don't really enjoy taking naps, and I really don't enjoy being by myself. So I can't identify with the desire to get up from the dinner table to go to my room and get away from the noise. I'm the opposite. I thrive in the noise and in the chaos. There aren't many days of fathering my girls when I would want to check out or get a moment alone—not physically, at least.

But just like Wynter, there have been plenty of days when I was unhappy, discontent, and not feeling the love and interactions in my home. I have often struggled in the life of my mind, and it can be very easy for me to nose-dive into the pits of sorrow, self-pity, and aggravation. And though there are multiple sources for my mental nosedives, the one place where the symptoms will manifest themselves is in my home—and with my girls.

But my isolation looks different from Wynter's and manifests itself in a few different ways.

For one, it can look like silence. I can easily be so consumed with self-pity that I spend an entire meal rehearsing my mood and misery in my head, leaving my girls to wonder what's wrong with Daddy and why he is so sad.

Or it can look like a short temper. For example, one of my girls might run up behind me and jump on my back, and I will respond in the wrong way. On the occasions when I've reacted poorly, I was actually aggravated at myself for a boneheaded decision I made (that really didn't matter in the grand scheme of things).

But the least noticeable, dullest, and yet negatively impactful habit is multitasking. Don't get me wrong—multitasking can be a good thing. Like when I'm doing the dishes while helping the kids with homework or when I'm driving my kids to school while we talk about a tough time one of my daughters is having with her teacher. But it can also become a bad habit prompted by the same emotion Wynter described when she wanted to be alone in the room—a desire to silence the noise.

Let me give you an example. One of my favorite things to do is listen to talk radio. Christian talk, conservative talk, liberal talk, sports talk, news talk…literally, it's my favorite way to pass the time. It's a completely normal thing to do when you're home alone vacuuming the floors or mowing the lawn. But between the hours of five p.m. and nine p.m., when my kids need me most, it's just escapism and laziness.

Acknowledging these flaws has caused me to bring them before the Lord in repentance. I turn them over to God because I want to connect with my daughters on a deeper level.

Before having my girls, I always wondered what it would be like to really connect with them and to know them. I even remember a bit of remorse and shame for not feeling close to them in the womb. I sort of envied Wynter during her pregnancies because what seemed to be natural for her was not kicking in for me. It was as if Wynter had this automatic, innate bonding with our girls while they were in the womb that just plain evaded me. Her maternal sense of intimacy seemed to start from the moment she found out she was pregnant, but it took me a full 38 weeks with the first two girls to even think about their entry into our world as imminent. Just in case you are wondering, they were both born at 38 weeks, so it took me experiencing their birth to really come to terms with my new reality and the new precious girls we had been given.

I remember moments when Wynter was talking to our daughters before they were born, reading to them, and daydreaming about them as if they were already among us. She knew them from the very beginning of her pregnancies. For me, growing in intimacy with my girls has been a gradual and continual process, and I suspect the same is true for most dads.

Now many more years into fathering, I find much joy in the intimacy and relationship I have with my girls despite my weaknesses mentioned above. One of the ways God has taught me how much my presence matters is through reflection and gratitude. He has motivated me to mentally "check in" when my mind tries to pull me away. So, as often as I can, I try to thank the Lord for each of my daughters. If I start to make a list, it can get pretty long pretty fast, so I like to think about the things I'm thankful for about my girls in two categories—tangible ties and soul ties.

There are many physical things that I thank God for, and these are the tangible ties. I'm thankful that I can reach out and hug them on a daily basis. When I'm traveling and not able to do this, I literally feel as if I'm missing a part of myself. I'm thankful that I can go to their volleyball games and gymnastics practices. There's just something that stirs my heart when I watch my girls in competition. I want to see them winning even more than I wanted to win when I was their age. I'm also thankful that I have the opportunity and privilege to discipline each of them, as correction is needed. Finally, I'm thankful that I can feel their hands tugging on my arms and their knees digging in my thighs as they climb into my lap, reminding me that my presence is wanted.

Eventually, I also began establishing soul ties. My girls became a lot more than just little bodies, and I began to get to know their real essence. As cute as they were, it was their minds and their interactions with the world around them that drew me into a deeper relationship with them. In the infant stages, that connection started with their facial expressions. After a few months of life, they smiled and cooed during the good moments and threw downright angry tantrums when they didn't get what they wanted. I still remember the joy in my heart when I realized for the first time that my presence made a difference and brought my daughters internal comfort and peace.

I remember it like it was yesterday. One of my girls would scream for what seemed like hours because of gas in her tummy or because we finally moved her into her own bedroom and she couldn't sense our presence. In a moment of desperation, I would go into her room, scoop her up, and pat her back. I had a favorite way of holding my girls with their face on the inside of my elbow, their tummy along my forearm, as my hand wrapped around their bottom and through their legs. I think I started holding them this way, sort of like a football, because it was the most comfortable and most natural way of holding them. You know, a very selfless reason!

Over time it developed into more than just my staple carry. It became the position I would hold them in to remind them that I was still close. For a moment they would scream, but a few minutes later my company would give them enough calm and relief to finally give up and fall asleep. They would let out a few last breaths and would then become comatose.

Amid these moments of joy and pain for my girls, and amid their recognition of my presence, I reached a second level of gratitude. I saw an appreciation in their eyes, not only for what I could do for them, but also for what I meant to them. Yes, I fed them, changed them, and met their basic needs, but now they recognized my presence and cognitively valued what I brought to their world.

I have no doubt that as you read this book, you realize you are needed. From the morning to the afternoon and late into the evening, your daughter reminds you on a regular basis that she depends on you. And although those needs change with each stage of girlhood, they never go away. But what about being wanted? Do you struggle with pulling back from your daily view of drop-offs and activities in order to consider how much you are wanted for who you are beyond what you can do for your daughter? In some stages of raising her it might be hard to tell that she values you, especially through the preteen years when it can seem as if her hormones are playing tricks on her!

Whether or not you feel it and whether or not you think *she* feels it is really beside the point. God created you for deep and intimate relationship with her. In the times when you can feel it, enjoy it! Your presence matters, and you should find joy being with her. When you aren't feeling it, engage. Let your emotions catch up with your feet, and watch what God does to deepen your relationship and influence in her life. This is a part of the journey where we must choose to be present. You are needed, and your presence matters.

——————————— LET'S PRAY ———————————

Lord,

It is easy to see that my daughter needs me, but it is sometimes difficult to see why. Because I'm always doing things for her and figuring things out for her, I can become so focused on my responsibilities that I forget that my daughter wants a relationship with me. Help me to remember that my presence matters more than what I do, what I accomplish, and how I help.

May I choose to connect to her world whether I feel it or not. Thank You for the moments when I do feel like it. Help my emotions to catch up with my feet when I don't. May I push aside my selfish tendencies and weaknesses to find joy in her presence, just as You pushed aside the outward signs of Your deity to rescue me in the middle of my humanity.

She is Yours, and I trust You with her.

Amen.

9

YOUR INTENTIONALITY

JONATHAN | One of my favorite things to do with my girls is to lie on the floor in one of their bedrooms while they all draw tattoos on my body. Either right before bedtime or on a lazy afternoon at home, I plop down on my belly. After what seems like hours, mainly because it is a good naptime for me, I end up with a flower, a block-letter name, a few random designs, and a bunch of long lines running down my arms and legs. I usually have two girls straddling my back, one on an arm, and another creating temporary tats on my calves.

Imagine me lying on the carpet facedown, enjoying the massage-like feeling of each pen running down my skin. A few daughters are gentler than their sisters, and every once in a while I wince in pain when a sharp pen tip nicks the tender part of my neck or side. There are not many words exchanged. That is, no one is exchanging words with me. My girls are always talking to each other as they coordinate their positions for the most creative collage—but for me, I experience an empty mind and a warm heart as my girls use me up for their own creative purposes.

Though I typically pass out during this time, my daughters will routinely have arguments about which one of them "owns" my right shoulder blade for the day and who gets to color in my fingernails. Sometimes my skin gets pinched by one of their little knees, or I'll get kicked in the back of the head, but it is barely noticeable as I lie there. I'm mesmerized by the closeness to them and the soothing nature of the process. In the midst of the chaos, I sometimes even smile, pray, and thank the Lord for the entire thing. It is a special treat indeed. I think I will inquire about one tomorrow!

I'll never forget waking up one morning after the previous evening's art session. In my relaxation, I put my girls to bed and swiftly went to bed myself, forgetting the evening's activity sheet that was my body. I woke in the morning to Wynter gasping at the black ink smeared into our new white bedsheets. If you know Wynter, you know that dirty, stained, or blemished sheets are one of her biggest pet peeves. It was not one of my finer moments from her perspective. Suffice to say, I took regular showers from that point forward after the Pitts girls' art class.

I long for opportunities to be close to my girls. There is nothing more exciting than when one of them plops in my lap on the couch. Just recently I had all three of "the littles" (yes, I will always call them my littles)—Kaitlyn, Camryn, and Olivia—in my lap on the couch, watching football. It was like a dream come true!

As my girls have grown, our tattoo sessions happen less frequently. But the art is the thing I miss the least. I miss the proximity more. I miss the messiness. I miss the scratches. I even miss the bumps and bruises that those activities brought with them, because they reminded me of our intimate times together.

Nowadays I have to be much more intentional about finding time, energy, and opportunities to be close to my girls. School, sports, camps, and technology—the worst offender—try their collective hardest to keep us from spending regular, deliberate, and focused time together. I'm forced to get creative and plan ahead to take advantage of even mundane opportunities to spend time with each of my daughters.

With four girls, this can be tricky, so I've learned to take what I can get. I set high expectations, as my earliest daddy dates were extravagantly planned and included dinners, movies, ice-skating, donuts, and so on. Expensive and time-consuming, this obviously has to be occasional. Though I still do these from time to time, I have learned to settle for a quick trip to the grocery store or even the hardware store. Surprisingly, they seem to enjoy this time just as much, and though a bit inconvenient—it will take me twice as long to grab lightbulbs or bread—the time is well worth it as I get more one-on-one time with each of them, and they seem to be vulnerable and open with me in the car and in the store.

Intentionality does not have to be expensive, time consuming, or stressful. It just requires you to think more creatively about how to incorporate time with your daughter into regular life—even when it seems a bit inconvenient.

WYNTER | I am not exactly sure when it happened, but one day I woke up and realized that my oldest daughter and I were standing eye to eye. I knew it was bound to happen, being that I stand right at five feet tall!

Initially this new vantage point felt strange. However, her height is just the evidence of what I already knew to be true. She is growing, and so are her sisters. They are becoming taller, wiser, and more mature. I love observing them as their hearts expand and wrap around others. I love seeing their strength, watching their beauty, and witnessing their development.

No matter how tall my girls get, there is one thing I love to do. I love to hold their hands. This simple act has been and continues to be a potent form of understanding between us.

Think about it. Holding hands is how our journeys begin. From the first day we meet our little bundles, we place a finger into the palm of their hand and wait for the moment we feel their tiny grasp. It is from that moment on that we are immediately and eternally connected to our girls.

For months we held hands while she ate, while she slept, and while she silently absorbed the new world surrounding her. At one year old, we held hands as she wobbled across the playground trying to find her own strength. At three years old, as she became too independent to be strapped down, we held hands as we strolled aisles and sidewalks together, searching for things we needed and a few things we just liked. At six years old, we held hands as she, full of excitement and uncertainty, boldly entered a room full of unfamiliar faces and took her place at the seat marked with her name. At the tender, awkward, and vulnerable age of ten, we held hands as she sought to find her place in the world of tweens. Now as we embark upon the twists and turns of her teen years, we hold hands while we talk, while we read, while we pray, and sometimes while we just sit quietly, snuggled on a couch in an empty room.

Often, holding hands in the midst of unsorted emotions becomes our silent language and a secret weapon that takes me right to the tender places of her heart. So I am committed to holding on.

I hold her hand because I want her to know that no matter how tall she gets, I am still here—loving her, guiding her, praying for her, protecting her, and comforting her. When she needs to talk, when she is ready to talk, I am within arm's reach, holding her hand just like the day we first met.

The world—her friends, her teachers, our society—is ready and waiting for the opportunity to grab our daughters' empty hands.

Steve Farrar talks about this in his book *Finishing Strong: Going the Distance for Your Family.* He uses the illustration of trying to score a perfect 300 in bowling and how much harder it is to do the further you stand away from the pins. He reminds us that knocking down all those pins is near impossible from the regulation line, but the closer you get to the pins, the better success you will have in knocking them all down. He ends with this awesome quote that brings the point home: "Error increases with distance. It's true with bowling, and it's true with families."

"Error increases with distance. It's true with bowling, and it's true with families."

STEVE FARRAR

So will you join me? No matter how old your daughter is, she will always need you close by. For confidence, for strength, for hope, for forgiveness, for encouragement—find a way to hold on tight. Yes, it takes effort. It takes humility. It takes understanding. It takes patience. Most of all, it takes intentionality. Without your intentionality, she will begin to pull away from you as a natural step of independence. It is your job to keep the distance to a minimum, decreasing the margin for error.

Though independence is normal with maturity, your daughter will never outgrow the need to hold a hand. I pray you don't let go. And as you hold her hand and guide her heart, continue to hold on tight to the hand of your heavenly Father.

Sometimes their maturity and growth can bring challenges and time constraints on how we spend time together. Here are some ideas and opportunities we've found to make spending intentional time together fun and meaningful.

"Yet I am always with You; You hold my right hand. You guide me with Your counsel, and afterward You will take me up in glory."

PSALM 73:23-24 HCSB

Ideas to Stay Close to Your Girl

1. Find a neighbor, a friend, church member, or even a stranger whom you can serve! Perhaps you could prepare a meal, clean a closet, or babysit their kids or pets.

2. Start a journal together. Secretly write notes to each other and hide the journal in a place where she will eventually find it (in her drawer, under a pillow, or in her backpack). When she finds it, she will write a note back to you and hide it. Make this an ongoing treat!

3. Take a picture walk. Go to a beautiful or cool place and take pictures while you talk.

4. Relax together with a mani-pedi at home or at a salon. (Dad, you can do this too. It's a good excuse to do what you've always wanted to do anyway!)

5. Find a local place with cool, pretty pottery pieces to paint!

6. Attend a concert or local event together. Choose something or an artist that she enjoys and invite yourself into her world!

7. Make new memories while remembering past experiences together by creating a scrapbook.

8. Exercise. Do fun dance exercises, make home videos, attend a class, or even swim together.

9. Write a creative story together. For example, let her write the first three sentences, and you write the next few. Continue developing the characters and plot by finishing where each of you left off.

10. Choose a recipe from online or an old family book and cook together.

11. Invite her to be a part of your everyday grown-up life. You might take her to work with you, run a few errands together, or go to an appointment or fancy "grown-up" business meeting. I (Jonathan) take my girls to my office at least once a week, and they love it! It makes them feel a part of my world too.

12. Choose a fun book, devotional, or book of the Bible to read together. Do this often!

13. Pull out your favorite childhood board game and teach it to your children. Notice how they react to playing a game that isn't on a mobile device.

14. Share each day's highs and lows. "Today my high was meeting a new friend, and my low was getting three problems wrong on my spelling test."

15. Spend quality time on a nice long bike ride.

16. Pump up the music, let yourself loose, and dance! This is one of my (Wynter's) favorites!

17. Pack sandwiches, salad, fruit, or fun treats. Sit on the grass or somewhere pretty and have a picnic.

18. Go for a walk! Try taking a nature walk and collecting things along the way. Bring in flowers to dry and flatten them in a book. Or look for some other cool craft for the things you collect.

19. Find a challenging puzzle to put together.

20. Sign up to take a lesson doing something new. Take

a lesson on dancing, cooking, scrapbooking, or photography. Often, communities will host affordable lessons at local public schools or community centers for community members, so make sure you look into those opportunities.

21. Plan and throw a mother-daughter party for your family's closest mother-daughter friends. Or invite your friends to a party and let your daughter invite her friends so they can all get to know each other. Throw a fancy dinner party or a slumber party.

22. Craft day! Make holiday decorations, gifts, cards, home decorations, things for her room, whatever. Make it a regular weekly or monthly thing and stick to it.

23. Have a girlie movie night. You can never go wrong there!

24. Spend time together while you praise and worship. Make up a dance or movements to a praise or worship song and perform it for an audience—Dad, other siblings, or friends. Don't be shy!

25. Make something together—your own jewelry, apron, blanket, or artwork.

26. Give each other a complete makeover. Take pictures, have a fashion show, and celebrate your new looks!

27. Find a cozy corner, grab a blanket and some pillows, and just be together! No plan, no agenda—just time to let your hearts connect.

28. Spend time together making a list of places to see and things to do together! Create a schedule and enjoy researching ideas together.

29. Go out for tea or stay in and have a private tea party. (If you are a dad, just take her to a coffee shop for hot chocolate since you are likely not feeling the tea-party idea.)

30. Pray for each other. Be honest and share prayer requests or things that you are struggling with, and ask her to pray for you and vice versa. Make this a normal part of your life together.

Some of these ideas are more appropriate for some ages than others, but I hope this list provides a good starting point for you. My prayer is that it will inspire you to pull your daughter in close in the very near future. Feel free to come up with your own ideas and build traditions with your daughter along the way.

It's less about the activity and more about the time and proximity. Whatever you do, make sure that what you are doing is something that takes her specific personality and interests into account. She needs to know that you are interested in being a part of her world.

WYNTER | One of my favorite memories is picking Alena up from school and seeing a brand-new level of excitement in her eyes. I had no idea what was causing the extra bounce in her step, but I anxiously waited as she tossed her backpack inside and slid into her seat.

She was bursting, and I could not wait to hear why.

It was obviously a big deal—maybe a mended friendship, a good grade, or an earned privilege...I knew it was going to be good. Seconds after placing her belt across her lap, she opened her eyeglass case and pulled out a crumpled, gallon-sized plastic bag full of loose grass and...ladybugs!

She was beyond excited. She was captivated by their journey around the crumpled walls of their new home. She and her sisters giggled and passed the bag around from seat to seat until they had a chance to experience the phenomenon up close.

Ladybugs. Alena, the new pets' owner, watched carefully as the bag bounced around the minivan until it made its way safely back to her lap. Enthralled. Curious. Proud. Those were her emotions. Me? I was confused and a tad bit grossed out. Still, I decided to let it happen. I nodded and mumbled "ooh" a few times, but mostly I kept my eyes on the road and pretended my van was not full of tiny critters.

Have you ever decided to just let it happen? To let your girls follow a passion, a journey, or a course of action that made absolutely no sense to you? I did. To my surprise, this peculiar fire inside of her did not die out as quickly as I assumed it would. It lived. They lived. And I decided to join them. It wasn't a natural reaction for me. It required my best intentions and pushing past my desires in order to enter her world.

Within moments of walking into the front door of our home, I found myself online trying to figure out how to take care of ladybugs. I watched Alena. I let her follow the questions of her heart right to their answers. Together we hovered over my kitchen counter and watched them live. We fed them, tapped on their spotted shells, and removed their lost loved ones over time. It turns out ladybugs don't make great pets, but we tried.

Together.

So here is what I learned. When something sparks her attention and draws out a passion that you just don't get, let it happen. Your daughter needs to know you are with her. She needs to know that the things that ignite the inner parts of her heart are worth exploring. She needs to know that what matters to her, matters to you.

One day it will be a mended friendship, an earned privilege, or— dare I say—a boy. And I pray that you will be right there with her.

Your intentionality is a key to ensuring an intimate relationship with your daughter that will allow for maximum influence. The world and its influences will seek to fill any voids, so be proactive in keeping her hands full with yours.

──────────────── LET'S PRAY ────────────────

Lord,

I thank You for giving me my daughter. I thank You for giving me the opportunity to have a strong presence in her life. Thank You for reminding me that my presence matters. Continue to encourage my heart to be present—physically, emotionally, and mentally.

But more than that, Lord, I pray that You would remind me and encourage my heart to be intentional in our time together. Lord, give me a passion for the things that stir her passion. Give me a desire to invest in those things, showing her that I care about her world and want to invest in her. When I'm tired, give me energy. When I'm disinterested, give me fortitude.

Lord, bless my investment in her, that it would bring both of us great joy and build a foundation of trust and loyalty. May my commitment to pulling her close create a bond that will last through the tough times and ultimately bring about generational and eternal blessings.

Where I lack the insight and creativity to enter her world, may Your Holy Spirit give me the inspiration and wisdom needed to break through the barriers.

She is Yours, and I trust You with her.

Amen.

10

HER PROTECTION

JONATHAN | Recently our family was visiting a friend's house on the first cool, crisp Saturday of a new fall season. The smell of dying leaves was in the air, and I was preparing my heart for the single fall activity that I anticipate with joy each and every year: football! Professional, collegiate, and high school football—I love them all! As I sat on my friend's back porch enjoying the smell of burgers on the grill, I watched our children playing in his backyard as our wives sat inside having a conversation.

It brought joy to my heart to watch our girls play together. This family happens to be a perfect match for our family because they have four daughters about the same ages as ours.

As always when I am on duty, I spend the majority of my time scanning the area for a head count. As I looked around, I got a glimpse of Alena riding around their large lawn on a golf cart with their oldest, while Kaitlyn played on their swing set.

As I looked down from the high deck, I continued looking for the twins. For a second my mind relaxed because I noticed that they were smack-dab in my line of sight, but about fifteen feet below the deck I was seated on. But a moment later I froze with fear. They and their playmate were standing on top of a retainer wall that had about a ten-foot drop to the backyard. They were beginning to sit down and were weighing out whether they could sustain the leap. Mind you, they were barely four feet tall themselves at the time, so this was no small feat.

I immediately yelled out in concern, "No!" All three of them stopped in their tracks, waiting for my next direction—though they didn't move from their position, hoping I might change my mind.

My gut instinct was to react with a strong and loving, "Go find somewhere else to play," removing any chance of a broken leg on that day. After all, I was excited for an afternoon of college football, and a visit to the emergency room would not fit on the agenda! But before I could get the words out, I noticed that the ground below them sloped from left to right. The ten-foot drop at one end gradually reduced until the ground was level with the top of the wall at the other end. Where they were sitting and wanting to jump only looked about four or five feet from the ground.

When I realized the height of the wall, I decided that the jump looked doable. I made the decision to allow them the freedom to jump. I decided the experience they would gain would be valuable for the next retainer wall they might sit on someday, without me there to monitor the situation. My role is not always to step in for the sake of avoiding risk altogether, but rather to provide the wisdom that guides them through the experience safely.

WYNTER | I don't know what it is with our girls and jumping, but I remember another similar episode from a few years before this one.

"Daddy, can you come here? I need your strong arms!"

Jonathan darted into the room to see just how he could save the day. About four steps past the entry of the doorway, he was greeted by five pillows strategically scattered around the floor and two pairs of eyes looking up—those of our twins, Camryn and Olivia, who were five years old at the time. Above him he heard the voice of our fearless Kaitlyn, then seven years old, saying, "Okay, Daddy, you may have to catch me," with excitement in her voice.

He stopped in his tracks and quickly looked up.

"Kaity, what are you doing?" he asked, as she hung over the banister of our staircase, no less than twelve feet from the lower level.

She casually replied, "I'm going to jump, but in case it doesn't work, I want you to catch me!" She was grinning from ear to ear with perfect peace. Did I mention Kaitlyn is fearless?

As you can imagine, Jonathan asked her to come down and explained to her the danger of jumping off a high ledge.

She was devastated.

In her mind, she was being brave. Everyone likes to feel brave, right?

She was being safe by asking her daddy to be there. We quickly moved on to another activity in hopes that Kaitlyn would never attempt to fly without us by her side!

In both cases I'm reminded of the importance of another of our primary roles in our homes: protection. Isn't that what a parent's love is really about? Stopping us before we try to jump too far, take a step that's too risky, or make a decision that could break us.

Just like my husband, God doesn't simply stand there waiting for us to fall; He guides us to safety. Just as Kaitlyn did with her daddy, our girls should trust our arms to catch them while they listen for our voices to lead them.

In the previous few chapters, we talked about being present and being intentional about growing our intimacy with our girls. We talked about finding joy, which is a wonderful thing. But while joy is a by-product of building a trust relationship, there are other more important reasons for building trust through intimacy. And protection is at the top of the list. When our girls want to jump off a ten-foot wall, we need to be there to stop them or to guide them to a lower section. When they have to get on the Internet for school projects, we need to be there to set the parameters. When they ask to go on their first sleepover or school dance, we need to be in their world enough to know whether the environment is appropriate. And as they move into their teenage years, we need to have a strong enough relationship with them to speak into every area of their life: boys, phones, jobs, insecurities, parenting, and everything else that is coming their way.

JONATHAN | I wish I could say these were the only stunts my kids have tried to pull off over the years, but I would be lying. Many involved water, a few involved frogs, and one involved an eight-foot jump rope dangling from an eighteen-foot catwalk. "What?" they pleaded. "We won't fall, Daddy, we promise."

But no, there are many more coming, and most of the ones they will face in the future will have the potential to be less physical and more emotional.

One summer when Kaitlyn was nine, I watched as she attempted to make friends on a foreign playground in California as we visited some family. As we've mentioned, Kaity has a huge heart and an even bigger personality, and she immediately made friends with a girl about her age. They ran around the playground, doing various activities together, and it warmed my heart to see her in her boldness.

But my heart sank as I watched her new friend encounter two other girls that she knew well. One of the two looked at my Kaitlyn with a bit of disgust in her eyes and said to Kaitlyn's new friend, "Who is she?"

Kaitlyn looked at the girl who asked the question with a huge smile, waiting to be accepted into the group. Obviously embarrassed, Kaitlyn's new friend shyly said, "I don't know," ran off with the two girls, and left my daughter in her tracks.

It took everything in me not to intervene. It helped that I was in a strange place. The comfort I might have had at our home playground was not in me, so I was forced to let the scenario play out. I felt horrible for my daughter and wondered what her next move would be. I assumed she would cry and run into my arms, but within seconds she ran off to another play area and enjoyed the rest of her time at the park.

I would be naive to think that this wasn't a painful experience for my daughter. In that moment she wanted nothing more than to be accepted into the group. If I could have, I would have given anything to stop that moment from happening. But in retrospect I'm glad it happened. She was able to feel rejection in a limited and controlled way. Rejection is a pain that none of us wants to feel, but just like other pains, it can prove to be helpful for our growth.

In times like these, protection simply means comfort.

Whether emotional or physical, we often do all we can to prevent feeling hurt in our own lives. But as much as we have tried, if we are honest with ourselves, we must admit that we have a losing record in this battle. We have been hurt by strangers, friends, teachers, pastors, and many other people we have trusted.

Worst of all, many of us have been hurt by our parents. To their credit, most often that hurt is unintentional. Our parents are sometimes oblivious to the pain that they created. And just so you know, I'm not trying to be hard on all parents. Oftentimes we, in our own sin, project causes of pain on our parents and blame them for the effects of self-inflicted pain. The enemy is constantly at work, seeking emotions to wreck and relationships to destroy.

And so we grow up with our own set of "when I have kids…

(insert promise)." But eventually we discover that in our efforts to protect our kids from the hurts we experienced, we end up creating a whole new set of hurts in them because of our opposite but equally offensive actions.

Many of these hurts and pains are deep within us, and we bring them into our parenting journey. It is easy for us to wallow in them, and left unchecked, they stand to drag us down into all kinds of temptations. Depression and sadness. Anger and bitterness. Mistrust and anxiety. The list goes on and on.

The first thing we need to remember in our personal struggle with pain is made plain in Romans 5:3-5.

> "And not only this, but we also exult in our tribulations, knowing that tribulation brings about perseverance; and perseverance, proven character; and proven character, hope; and hope does not disappoint, because the love of God has been poured out within our hearts through the Holy Spirit who was given to us."
>
> **ROMANS 5:3-5** NASB

Thank the Lord, many of us have been freed from the chains of our pains! But if I had to guess, I would gamble that most of us, though liberated from a few, still have a few hangers-on.

I would encourage you to take this time to reaffirm your trust in the Lord to free you completely from the prison of your own resentment. Take this moment and this opportunity to ask the Lord, again or for the very first time, to show you the areas in your life where you are tied up in slavery. Ask Him to give you His strength in your weakness. Ask Him to do whatever He has to do to make you free.

The Lord can use your past pain for His glory. This is actually one of His favorite things to do. That is why the best person to help someone trapped in a struggle is someone that has been liberated from that same struggle.

The degree to which you get freedom in your own personal life will be to the degree to which your girls fully see freedom lived out and Christ shining the brightest in you. The greatest thing we can do to protect our girls from the pain of sin and strongholds is to seek freedom ourselves and watch how God uses our lives to speak to them.

This is an area that Wynter and I know all too well. We brought some of our own hurts and pains into our marriage and therefore into our parenting journey. We thought it best to stop here and take a moment to offer our pains, hurts, and guilt to the Lord.

But before we move on, let's stop and take a moment to think about this:

Have you decided how open you will be with your girls when they ask you questions about your past? Maybe I am alone in this, but today I pray that God would help me to lead an honest and transparent life that will welcome the burdens of others, including and most importantly those of my girls.

As much as I would like to shield my girls from every physical, emotional, and spiritual pain and danger lurking around them, I can't. I want to be there to protect them from every retainer wall, staircase, mean girl, and self-serving boy that attempts to bring harm their way, but it isn't practical or possible.

So instead I choose to thank the Lord for the times when I will be there. I choose to ask Him for His wisdom. I pray He shows me when to yank her out of the fire, when to help guide her

"It was for freedom that Christ set us free; therefore keep standing firm and do not be subject again to a yoke of slavery."
GALATIANS 5:1 NASB

through the danger, and when to sit back and trust that God is in control. Protecting our girls is not about being helicopter parents, overprotecting and having an excessive interest in their lives. Wynter and I are not advocating that you insert yourself in every area of your daughter's life in a way that prevents her from learning how to make decisions or shields her from the world around her.

Instead, we are suggesting and attempting ourselves to take enough interest in our daughters to not leave them on their own. We hope to do all we can to protect them, being responsible with the oversight God has given us and then trusting the Lord to do the rest. We pray that He gives us insight and wisdom as we trust Him to be Shepherd and Protector for all of us.

"Because you have made the LORD—my refuge,
    the Most High—your dwelling place,
    no harm will come to you;
    no plague will come near your tent.
For He will give His angels orders concerning you,
    to protect you in all your ways.
They will support you with their hands
    so that you will not strike your foot against a stone.
You will tread on the lion and the cobra;
    you will trample the young lion and the serpent.
Because he is lovingly devoted to Me,
    I will deliver him;
I will protect him because he knows My name."

PSALM 91:9-14 HCSB

─────────────── LET'S PRAY ───────────────

Father,

Thank You for Your great compassion and for cleansing me from my sin (Psalm 51:1-2).

Thank You for taking the guilt away and for restoring me to You.

Lord, as I humble myself where I have failed You, I ask that my broken spirit and repentant heart be direction and an example to my daughter. I pray that my compassion would be an open door for her to share her failings with me, and a reminder to her that she doesn't have to walk alone.

As she grows older, I'm becoming more aware of her fragility. I sense a need to protect her physically, emotionally, and spiritually.

One of the greatest fears I have for my daughter has to do with the possible pain and agony that awaits her in this life. Lord, I've not stopped worrying about her physical protection since the day she was born. But Lord, right now, I give that fear and anxiety to You.

I choose to trust Your hand, and I ask You to give me the wisdom and strength I need to protect her mind, body, and emotions.

Lord, I can't do enough devotions and I can't pray enough prayers to fence her in from the enemy's attacks. So I choose to trust Your hand, and I ask You to give me the wisdom and strength I need to guide her to Your loving arms.

Teach her to lean on Your great compassion.

Remind her that she has me and others with whom she can share her burdens, knowing that we will gently and lovingly point her toward Your grace.

Lord, she is Yours, and I trust You with her.

In Jesus's name, amen.

HER RELATIONSHIP WITH YOU—FINAL THOUGHTS

Years down the road, I imagine a conversation with one of my girls going something like this: "Mom, remember that time I brought home a bunch of ladybugs?" Silence. Immediately followed by an uproar of contagious giggles and uncontrollable laughter. "And how they all died one by one?"

I imagine our memories will serve as a reminder that we didn't do this perfectly, but we did it together, with our daughters.

As I think about my reality and my attempts at being present and pulling my girls close, I think about things like this. I'm the mom who...

- Buys a kit to create your own gum, only to burn it in the microwave.

- Takes three days and a slew of YouTube videos to figure out how to turn rubber bands into a beautiful work of art and a colorful accessory using a Rainbow Loom.

- Tries to bake an edible cookie bowl. I can't even think of the proper words to describe how horrifically this ended. Pure pandemonium as a party of ten girls tried to scoop ice cream into a pile of burnt crumbs.

- Paints nails...and cuticles.

- Always has to double the amount of suggested flour in order to stop the homemade play dough from becoming a permanent place mat.

- Forgets to turn on the oven light when making a Shrinky Dink, causing us to entirely miss the point— the shrinking.

- Successfully bakes reindeer cupcakes but then arrives too late to the class party, missing the unveiling and enjoyment of my labor.

And friends, this is just the beginning! I am serious. This list could go on and on! Regardless of my many failed attempts, my ultimate goal is to never stop adding bullet points. Let's just call it a work in progress.

The specific activities may not be my proudest parenting acts, but combined they are what define the most significant contribution I give to my girls. My time.

So, I imagine my daughters will have endless stories from their childhood, and I am prepared to be the punch line for most of them! However, it's the first few words of their stories that are the most important to me: "Mom, remember when..."

Memories are not defined by perfect scenarios. The present moment, the daily interactions, and the quality time we spend with our children will guide and provide the substance of future conversations.

Think About It

1. As you think about how much your presence matters, identify the scenarios and situations that most cause you to check out physically, emotionally, or spiritually from your daughter.

2. Your intentionality matters. Are you purposefully drawing close to your daughters? In what ways?

3. Your protection matters. Are you responsible with the voice, instinct, and authority God has given you over your daughter? In what ways?

PART 3

HER RELATIONSHIP WITH THE WORLD AROUND HER

HER RELATIONSHIP WITH THE WORLD AROUND HER— LET'S GET STARTED

We have spent a lot of time discussing what raising God's girls looks like inside the environments we create for them. We've talked about the impact we can have in our homes in regard to their relationships with us as their parents, and their relationship with God as their Creator. Now it's time to switch gears just a little.

What happens when our girls leave the house? Actually, as I type this, I am reminded that our daughters do not have to physically go anywhere to experience the impact of the world around them. Here are a few statistics to give a general overview of a few things we already know to be true.

- The average eight-year-old child spends eight hours a day on media. A teen typically spends more than eleven hours with media a day.

- In 2011, 36 percent of teens had a smartphone. In 2014, it grew to 79 percent.

- Kids thirteen to seventeen years old send an average of 3,300 texts per month.*

Unfortunately, we are not always there to guide, lead, or protect them. Our daughters need to know how to react and respond according to God's will in the world around them. Often we want specific answers to questions in relation to their environment. Decisions about when to allow social media into their life, how many hours of screen time they should have, and what age is the right age for sleepovers all involve careful consideration and prayer. However, in this section we would like for you to look beyond the details and at the broader scope of how we equip our daughters to walk through their decision making with a Christlike perspective.

In part 3 we will discuss your daughter's relationship with the outside influences that will inevitably force their way into her life. Let's examine your role as a parent as these forces begin to speak into her life.

---

* "Facts and TV Statistics," *Parents Television Council,* http://w2.parentstv.org/main/Research/Facts .aspx.

11

HER INFLUENCES

WYNTER | As a parent, I'd like to believe that my words, my actions, and the lifestyle lived in our home is what will have the biggest impact on the life of my daughters. But I am not completely naive. By the age of five, each of my girls had spent at least five hours a day under the influence of others. In the beginning it was mainly teachers and school administrators that had been carefully selected to lead the educational journey we'd chosen. Even in that, we were still sort of setting the environment, though we didn't have our hands on all the controls.

But with each passing day and year, the influences have become exponentially more in source and content. As much as we try, it is just impossible to ignore the fact that our girls' hearts and minds will be impacted by the world in which they live. Outside influencers are inevitable; therefore, our role is to teach our daughters to navigate them well.

I may not be able to control everything my daughters hear, see, and experience, but I can do my best to help guide how they process and maneuver through each situation.

I first learned the benefit of this way of thinking when one of our girls woke up after having a bad dream. It was dark and I was asleep, so some of the details are a little "iffy." I am assuming it was somewhere between midnight and five a.m. when our two oldest daughters, nine and six at the time, came storming into our room in a panic. Actually, it was probably just the nine-year-old in the panic, and her little sister wasn't really sure why she was hurrying into my bed. She and I were on the same page. Groggy and confused.

I could hear the commotion happening, but I could not balance my thoughts enough to respond. I was lost somewhere in that awkward place between good sleep and the realities of parenthood. Here's what I saw.

The confused daughter was sitting in the middle of my bed, patiently rocking herself while sucking her two fingers. The older one was panic-stricken. Tears were flowing excessively, and while words appeared to be coming out of her mouth, she just couldn't pull herself together enough to string them into a sentence. Her emotions had taken over.

Somewhere in the midst of trying to focus on the girls, I got a glimpse of my husband doing some sort of manly, protective, king of the jungle ritual. He hopped out of bed, ran to the bedroom door, skipped over to the window, fixed the blinds, jumped across to the other side of the bed, and mumbled, "Where's my bat?" He then took off to finish the routine in the living room.

At this point I sat up and asked, "What is wrong?"

My sweet girl replied, "I heard a squirrel crying in the creek."

As you can imagine, my initial response was utter confusion, but I was pretty sure my husband was responding to the exaggerated emotions of his baby girl rather than the realities of what was happening. He probably never even asked why she was so upset. Of course, to his defense, it was dark, and he was exhausted and barely awake.

However, our early morning drama caused me to think about what impact we have on how our girls process the world around them.

As parents it is our responsibility to provide them with the tools that help them process their experiences. It's important that we respond and react according to the reality of what is happening in their world and help them filter it through a biblical lens.

In addition to being a great story that Jonathan and I will recall for many years to come, it came with some unintended value. We've learned that the following steps will help our girls process the outside influences they will inevitably experience.

Listen to Her

Really listening to my daughter's explanation that night might have eased the tension and led to a very different and less eventful evening. We oftentimes respond to their body language, tone, or our immediate perception of the situation. Taking the time to listen might change everything in a moment.

Listening before interacting or reacting gives us a chance to really hear what they are truly experiencing as opposed to what we think they are experiencing based on our reality and perceptions.

Even in our home, each of our girls sees the world through a different lens, and part of being able to guide them is understanding where they are coming from.

Understand Her Environment

Our home backs up to a wooded creek, and the whole back wall of the house is glass. From my daughter's youthful vantage point, everything beyond those windows was magnified. Remembering this can help me put myself in my daughter's shoes and see things from her perspective. Knowing what is going on in your child's world will assist you in helping, responding, calming—really whatever the "ing" needs to be in that moment. Is she having problems with a friendship? Did she not sleep well last night? Understanding these variables will help you be somewhat more sensitive to her feelings so you can respond appropriately.

Both listening to our daughters and gaining an understanding of their environment helps us to better choose the appropriate tools to help their situation.

Using the same example, a baseball bat did absolutely nothing to solve our dilemma with the sad squirrel, but a hug probably would have done the trick. Figure out early what approach or tool might assist you in helping.

We are still figuring this out, but we have learned that with each of our daughters, within an array of scenarios, there can be countless responses requiring countless tools. The primary tool and one we always try to remember is prayer. Here are two common kinds of prayer in our household:

- *Fervent, continual, and regular prayer for wisdom.* We pray that God would guide us in helping our daughters to navigate and align their perspectives with God's as they process the influences in their lives.

- *Prayer in the moment.* There are times when you and I will enter a scenario where we have no idea how to respond or help our daughters. In moments like these we take a moment to pause and ask God for guidance. We also ask Him to guide our daughters. We have found that simply doing this, especially in very emotional situations, brings a level of calm and peace that is needed, in addition to God's perspective.

JONATHAN | As I contemplate my daughters, their environment, and the influences in their lives, I think about their friendships. Friends play a significant role in life, especially as we grow up. I pray for healthy, God-honoring friendships. I can't help but think about how I often failed in that area in my life growing up. Even as a young man who loved the Lord and was seeking Him, I still had a desire to fit in. More often than I should have, I went along with the crowd, being molded and shaped by those around me in an ungodly manner. Instead of being a Christlike friend and an incubator of His truth and grace, I often found myself doing just the opposite. As I think back on those days—from middle school through high school and into college—I can only praise God for being so faithful in the midst of my bad decisions. Also, I am filled with gratitude for parents who were prayer warriors who sought God on my behalf.

I'm not saying we shouldn't have friends who aren't Christ followers, but at the time, I should have made it my goal to only indulge in those relationships when I could have been the influencer instead of the influenced. On top of that, I should have looked to surround myself with people of greater character. I needed people who were further along in their faith, who would have been willing to pour into me.

Thank God that I had parents willing to go to God on my behalf. I have no doubt that their prayers were the ones that brought a high school football coach into my life who would call out my selfish nature—the coach who nicknamed me One Way (because I always wanted my own way) and challenged me to a deeper level of sacrifice in my friendships. And it was my parents' prayers that brought a godly young mentor and gospel choir director into my life who would speak prophetically to me when I was a knucklehead of the highest order. Now, though I rarely see them, I count them both lifelong friends who helped shape me into the man I am today.

May we be parents who seek the Lord on behalf of our girls, pleading and begging Him to intervene in their friendships and in their ability to be godly friends themselves.

May we also model what healthy friendship looks like. Think about your friendships— are any unhealthy for you or your friend? Are there close relationships in your life where you are modeling Proverbs 27:6, where you are willingly and boldly approaching your friends, appropriately encouraging them when necessary? Additionally, are you the type of friend who is open to being encouraged, challenged, and even reproved when necessary? Remember, your girl is always watching, listening, and absorbing. When you are on the phone or at a friend's house, does what you say and how you respond model healthy, God-honoring conversation that you would be willing for your daughter to imitate?

In addition to modeling true friendship and praying for their friendships, we need to do all we can to guide them along the way. I've learned to not judge their friends or make them feel bad for wanting to be friends with certain people. In the past I've tried this, and it does not work. At least, it hasn't for me. Telling them who they can and can't be friends with will likely cause resentment.

Instead, be intentional about getting to know their friends, and include their parents. Set up playdates and family dates, ask questions, and show your children that you are interested in helping them cultivate true friendships. And when you know that their friend isn't the type of person you want influencing your child, you always have the prerogative to limit the interactions that they have with them and set the boundaries around their interactions.

WYNTER | We have attempted to expand our daughters' horizons in friendship, exposing them to a larger tray of options, if you will.

You can do this by getting more involved in places where you know there will be much to gain from the experience.

For example, when the girls were young, as difficult as it was, we decided to serve together in an inner-city after-school program not many miles from our home. We committed to going once a week. Though we didn't go there with friendship in mind, it was an incredible by-product of our service. Our girls interacted with children of all ages at the center, befriending kids their age, older, and younger as they served. Interestingly, though our girls were helpful, they sort of merged into the program, adding the most value by being friends to be modeled. They learned what good friendship looks like from many of the kids at the program, as well.

> "God has not called us to raise safe kids; He's called us to raise strong ones. He hasn't called us to raise popular kids; He's called us to raise spiritually potent ones."
>
> **TIM KIMMEL**

Yes, broaden your girl's perspective and encourage her to have a wide variety of friends. Go as far as challenging her to befriend the new girl or the one who plays alone at recess. Often we have an idea of who we want our girls to be friends with—the smart, the athletic, the creative—but God has other things in mind for our daughters as they grow in relationships, so may we not limit our girls with our own personal bias.

As we model, as we pray, and as we guide, may we do so with God's perspective as we trust Him to do what we cannot.

The influences our daughters will face are more than we can name or even speak to in this short book, but thankfully, God has not left you or me alone to figure it out on our own. He has given us His Word, He has given us His Spirit, and He has given us each other. Let's discuss a few of those influences in the next few chapters.

——————————————— LET'S PRAY ———————

Lord Jesus,

Within every day and every situation exists the opportunity for my daughter to be influenced by someone or something. May I not look at this reality with fear or anxiety, but as an opportunity to bring my influence and Your truth to bear on her life, teaching and training her how to process all the information, advice, and temptations that will come her way.

Help me to be a voice of calm, bringing emotions down when necessary.

Help me to be a compass, pointing her toward true north as she goes along the way.

Help me to be an ear of understanding, never standing in judgment, but ready to bring correction.

Help me to be wise, making the most of every opportunity You give me to grow her when other influences look to set her back.

Help me to devote the time and energy needed to be real with her as she brings her gratefulness, excitement, worries, fears, and anxieties to You. Help me to do my part while remembering that…

She is Yours, and I trust You with her.

Amen.

12

HER TIME

WYNTER | I assumed that once the four girls were out of diapers, the busyness of life would begin to settle down. I was wrong.

It's actually more like this: Once the diapers came off, we immediately filled the water bottles, put on the cleats and leotards, threw a ball in the car, and headed to the gym or the field!

I love being a soccer mom, a basketball cheerleader, and even a concert photographer, but keeping up with my girls' schedules can result in a busy life with little time left over to focus on the things we value the most—our personal relationships and our spiritual growth.

We have found that if we are not intentional about what activities we allow our kids to be a part of, we find ourselves exchanging quick goodbyes over fountain drinks and ketchup packs. Jonathan will be headed to the right with a few of our girls, while I head to the left with whoever remains!

Being involved in extracurricular activities is a valuable aspect of raising well-rounded and responsible girls, but we are forever working to keep the main thing the main thing. Yes, there are seasons of life that are just plain busy, but we try not to make it the norm.

With the many tempting and exciting activities for our girls to explore and master, deciding when to say no is a necessity, though doing so can be challenging and heartbreaking.

Choosing the right activities for your family requires careful consideration, wisdom, and prayer. But for the sake of guarding how your daughter spends her time, you must set boundaries and choose to live within them.

One of the first conversations Jonathan and I had as newlyweds was with a mature couple we respected. I reflect on the concepts they presented to us as they shared how their family spent their time. We, too, have tried to incorporate their wisdom into our family's values.

- Every good opportunity is not for you. Set your goals and measure your opportunities against the direction your family is headed.

- Take time together to reevaluate where you are headed. Consider what's important to you.

- Pray for direction.

I'd like to offer you this same wisdom.

Resist the urge to do it all. In our home we have set a "one activity or sport per child at a time" rule. (Yes, that's all I can handle!) It is important to decide how much you and your family can handle without losing focus on the things that matter most.

Of course, this decision is one only your family can make, and you can customize it depending on your family's values and circumstances. If your daughter happens to be on the Olympic gymnastics team, it's going to look a whole lot different for you to prioritize your time than it does for us.

Discuss your family's schedules. Before you plan out your calendar, decide what you are not willing to do. That might look like deciding that whatever extracurricular activities you commit to, you *will* have an average of two or three quality-time dinners a week together as a family. If you don't set your boundaries, they will be set for you.

This takes intentionality. Treat your family calendar the same way you do your work calendar or your own social calendar. The things that you prioritize will happen. The things you wish to happen tend to drift without your best efforts and organization.

Study your children and pray for direction. As parents it is our responsibility to know our children's bent. Spend time learning what your children enjoy doing, what they are good at, and what matters to their hearts. Seek out opportunities that match who God created them to be.

Going back to the Olympic gymnastics illustration, you can have the best intentions in the world in signing your daughter up for the competitive gymnastics class, but most likely your children and mine are not the next Simone Biles. You need to ask yourself if the time you are spending on activities for your children is worth the cost and lost opportunity in other areas.

"Pay careful attention, then, to how you walk—not as unwise people but as wise—making the most of the time, because the days are evil."

EPHESIANS 5:15-16 HCSB

Lastly, make sure you are taking the time to seek the Lord for wisdom. You have a limited amount of time to spend with and disciple your children. Always be willing to consider changing your family plan and boundaries to make the best use of your time.

JONATHAN | I liken our family calendar to our financial budgeting. When push came to shove, there didn't seem to be anything that could budge, but having the wherewithal to pay attention and make different decisions ultimately resulted in a better prioritization. We valued our spiritual investment over the physical, though we are still a work in progress in this area. And just like in our budgeting, God's grace ultimately answered prayers and reminded us that even our best efforts need His special touch.

First, God put Wynter and me on the same page with a desire to invest our time. Starting with the time we already had in our home, we began to turn off the television and utilize our time together at weeknight dinners and Saturday breakfasts. We committed to holding at least three family devotions each week, utilizing our dinnertime as often as possible, and doing more when we could. We would make sure to pray and read Scripture together as a family before leaving home for school or our day's activity, among other things. We still don't do this perfectly, but budgeting the time has helped us become more consistent investors in the hearts and minds of our girls on a routine basis.

Second, God brought along a few support systems, including a Bible learning and memorization program that happened on Sunday nights a half mile from our home. The program took place at a Christian school that would invest in our children spiritually and provide a place for our girls' activities to be held. No longer were we running from town to town like before! Though we are still working through this, we chose to centralize our activities, and the ones that didn't fit within a few central zones (church and school primarily) were deprioritized.

Lastly, God graciously gave us a spiritual community—a church that would support everything that we were teaching our girls at home. Though this one sounds like the easiest commitment, it has proved the hardest because it requires sacrifice from us. Nevertheless, we decided that this time commitment was a worthy investment. In addition to finding a church family that you sense is the right fit for your children, you have to agree to show up.

When our daughters decided to join the church Christmas choir, it meant rehearsals. Long ones. And a lot of them.

When they were invited to be a part of the youth leadership team, it meant early Sunday morning alarm clocks. (Neither of us are early morning people, so this one hurt.)

When one of our girls joined the youth worship team, it meant midweek rehearsals and multiple Sunday services, and for me, it meant missing the first half of Sunday football. Talk about budget cuts!

Was it a sacrifice? Yes. But we made and make these decisions knowing that the small investment now will reap much larger benefits later. We had to learn to value these eternally focused activities over the more temporal.

Do I sometimes question whether I'm blocking my daughter's ability to make the Olympic soccer team? Sometimes. But if she makes the Olympic soccer team but fails to grow in her relationship with Christ, what has she gained?

Think about your family and the doors God has opened. Think about other doors that you knocked down that are draining more out of your time budget than you can afford to give. Do you need to make any decisions today that will help you refocus and prioritize your time with your daughter and your family? Are you committed to investing in your daughter spiritually?

With our time within our homes, our communities, and our churches, may we invest in things eternal and pray that God blesses the sacrifice and desires of our heart. May we prioritize activities that nurture their relationship with Christ and bring maximum benefit to them and our family.

"Seek first the kingdom of God and his righteousness, and all these things will be added to you."
MATTHEW 6:33 ESV

——————————————— LET'S PRAY ———————————————

Father,

As I think about my time, my family's time, and my girls' time, I can't help but be overwhelmed by how quickly it passes. There are so many things that I want to do, that I want our family to do, and that I want my girls to do. But we can't do it all. So, Lord, instead of getting overwhelmed by the never-ending list of possible to-dos and activities available, may I begin to prioritize the things You prioritize.

Starting in my home, may I see it as a place where we multiply our collective investment in making much of Your name. May I teach my girls what it looks like to have a household devoted to growing in understanding and godliness. May You bless my efforts, as feeble as they may be, and give me and my daughters joy in the process.

In our communities, may we look to make the most of our days, fully committed to utilizing our time to shine the light of Jesus into the darkest of places. In our sports clubs, in our dance academies, and in neighborhoods, may our time be multiplied for the good of those we come in contact with.

May my family be intimately involved with the body of Christ, Your church. Stretch us and grow us through our time spent together, and utilize our gifts to serve in whatever capacity You've provided.

Lord, help me to seek You first, and help me to train my daughter to seek You first in all things, knowing that how she spends her time will greatly influence her heart for You.

She is Yours, and I trust You with her.

In Jesus's name, amen.

13

HER HEART TO SERVE

JONATHAN | Growing up in a charismatic Christian home, my life was filled with church activity. Most weeks I would find myself at the church for at least three activities and sometimes four. Sunday morning worship and some sort of Sunday evening experience were a given. And for some reason, my family was on a normal schedule for cleaning the church, which could have doubled our time there. My siblings and I weren't thrilled, but we learned hard work and responsibility. I still remember the distinct smells of the dust in the basement and the moist bathrooms. I also remember the breaks that my brother and I would sneak in when we were sent to take the trash to the Dumpster or to do anything outside. We would drag our feet as long as we could in order to savor the fresh air and the moment away from the tasks at hand.

While all those great memories and activities shaped who I am today, there is one Christian activity I will never forget: feeding the homeless. I don't remember how old I was when I started or exactly when my service came to an end, but how long I served has proven to be insignificant. I had an experience with serving "the least of these" that would change my world. My parents exposed me to the needs of the poor and the vulnerable through this opportunity. I grew up with very humble means, and I thought we were poor, but my service to those in need reminded me of the wealth we had. I gained perspective and appreciation for God's provision while simultaneously coming to value the riches of knowing Christ Jesus and God's goodness.

There were other service activities that I was involved in along the way, like lawn maintenance for the elderly and various helps for sick and shut-in persons in my church. I was also a Boy Scout, achieving the Eagle Scout award, the highest achievement possible in the scouting program. It was in the Boy Scouts that the Bible would come alive most as I sought to "do my duty to God and my country." We did road cleanups, served at dinners, organized community service projects, and much more, all of which expanded my understanding of and commitment to serving others. These service opportunities had a real impact on my understanding of what it meant to follow Jesus Christ in action, not just in word.

"Truly I tell you, whatever you did for one of the least of these brothers and sisters of mine, you did for me."

MATTHEW 25:40

Serving and helping those who couldn't help themselves was ingrained in my DNA and tethered to my faith. I knew the Scriptures well, and thankfully I had parents who made the Word come alive.

WYNTER | My experience with service was not all that different from Jonathan's. While we too spent a lot of time serving in ministries at my church, it would be my mother's heart in the streets, literally, that would have the greatest impact on my childhood.

My mother is one of the most selfless and generous people I know. If you met her today, I would warn you to not compliment her on her shirt because one would probably show up in your mailbox soon after your visit. She really is just that giving!

As a little girl, this always struck me as odd because in the eyes of most we did not have much to offer. I grew up in a row home in the inner city of Baltimore, Maryland. My father spent most of my childhood struggling with drug addiction, which left my mother alone with the financial pressure of raising my brother and me. We moved in with my grandmother after my mother and father were divorced. As I have shared previously, despite these unfortunate circumstances, my childhood was rooted in and dependent upon faith in God. This very dependency would serve as the catalyst to my mother's selflessness. She was fully aware of her inability to provide for herself and claimed no ownership of the little she had. Whenever she crossed paths with people in need, she eagerly shared with them.

My mother never hesitated to buy a meal for a friend or a stranger. As a little girl, I remember driving on rainy days and pulling over to offer women and children a ride to their destination, even if it was in a different direction from ours. My brother, grandmother, and I would squeeze in tight as my mother would hop out of the driver's seat and help to load strollers, bags of groceries, and dripping-wet toddlers into our small vehicle.

I never knew how to process her extremely selfless acts. It would take me some time to fully understand, but now I know just how much God's grace in her life drove her selflessness. She was giving out of gratitude, and her giving was an offering back to the Lord for what He had done for her.

JONATHAN | There was a common thread that ran through our childhoods for which we are grateful. Our parents owned their zone! They saw the influence that the Lord had given them and the gifts and resources they had, modest as they were, and they brought those things to bear in the situations God had dropped them in. Despite our childish complaints and grumblings, they still brought us along for the ride (literally in Wynter's case!).

In our parenting journey so far, we have looked for areas where the Lord is calling us to give of our time, talent, and treasure; specifically, to help children and families within our sphere of influence. We've sometimes gotten it right, and we have oftentimes gotten it wrong, but we are thankful that the Lord has opened doors wide to help us out. We need only to walk through them—and take *our* kids along for the ride!

"Therefore, I urge you, brothers and sisters, in view of God's mercy, to offer your bodies as a living sacrifice, holy and pleasing to God— this is your true and proper worship."

ROMANS 12:1

One such God-ordained place that our family plugged into and served for five years was a small after-school program in the inner city of Dallas. I was a few months into a new job when one of my staff members walked into my office and said, "Hey, I want you to meet some people." It was a busy day for us, but I agreed to walk in and meet whoever was in my conference room.

I was greeted by a husband and wife. They had a new ministry that was providing after-school care, tutoring, and meals to a large group of disadvantaged youth in one of the poorest neighborhoods in our city. They had been business owners but had decided to sell their business and go recklessly after the call that God had put on their hearts. They were caring for the welfare of the city in which God had planted them—and their work was growing!

Having served full-time in ministry for more than seven years at

that point, I had run into hundreds of ministries already with awesome missions, so it wasn't out of the ordinary. I thought this ministry wanted something from the organization at which I worked,
and I was waiting for the catch. But the couple really wasn't there for
that purpose. They were invited to my office, seemingly randomly,
and so they had come.

As the couple began to talk about what they were doing, I was
enamored with their decision to leave behind unimaginable success in business to pursue a "roll up your sleeves" ministry like after-
school care in the inner city. They described the conditions of the
community, the brokenness of the families they were serving, and
the program in detail as I homed in on what they were doing.

Knowing that Wynter grew up in a very similar community, and
taking note of the couple's charisma, I became inquisitive enough to
ask for more information. So we decided to make a visit—Wynter,
our girls, and I. The older girls were eight and six at the time, and
the twins were three. It's a little embarrassing looking back, because
if I were in their shoes, I would have judged my family to be more
of a burden than a help. Four kids eight years old and under coming to serve? I don't even know what we were thinking!

We went for a visit and kept coming back. It was a weekly experience for our family for most of those five years, and we became
friends with the people God called us to serve and the volunteers.
The couple that started the place are dear friends to this day, and
those folks became a real and heaven-sent part of our world.

I'll never forget the clumsiness of our visits for the first few
months. First of all, at three years old, the twins were one year
younger than the kids who attended the program. They were effec-
tively squatters! I remember getting the volunteer sign-up form that
stated their policy of a minimum age of four years old for kids and
wondering, "Should my family not be here?"

To make matters worse, my kids weren't supposed to be served because we were a volunteer family, but somehow they always ended up falling among the ranks of the children showing up for fellowship, games, tutoring help, and meals. We were supposed to be serving. I was completely self-conscious about it, but the couple brushed it off as if it was no big deal. They never treated our kids like a bother, and they encouraged us to keep coming back. And though our other two girls at eight and six were a bit older, they were still some of the younger kids in the bunch, so they were not yet much help either.

When we first got there, Wynter and I spent more time wrangling our own kids than helping others. It was intense. We began planning before we would arrive, deciding which one of us would manage our kids so the other could serve. That lasted a few months before we noticed that our kids were becoming family and friends to the children there.

We felt like a bother, but they treated us like family. We didn't feel like we were much help, but soon we realized that God was using us from the very beginning. I'll never forget one time when the couple leaned over to thank us for putting ourselves through chaos to be there each week. Honestly, we would have likely been discouraged and quit if not for their encouragement. They said that for the kids we were serving, we were a rare portrait of an intact family. You see, most of the children came from family brokenness, abuse, and neglect. Our family, though far from perfect, stood in stark contrast to that.

Over time, all the girls integrated into the program, befriending the other children and becoming a part of what we found to be a large family. Sometimes our big girls would blend in with the other kids, but soon we found them tutoring kids in their grade levels and below. Over time, they tutored kids ahead of them in grade level because many of the kids were so far behind. By the time we left, Alena was leading the girls club with Kaitlyn as her sidekick.

We left discouraged on many days, believing we hadn't worked enough. I was sometimes upset because I didn't get to talk about Jesus with any children that day. Nonetheless, the Lord was using our family and our drama. Children with distorted views of God's order saw what marriage and family looked like when done God's way—in His order. It was one thing for the program to teach it, but it was something different to model it.

This story is a long way of reminding you that God has created you, your daughter, and your family with purpose in mind. God has plans for you now that include your daughter, so never underestimate what He can do if you make yourself available to Him now. If you stay in a posture of availability, God will open your eyes to the needs around you and give you a compassion for scenarios and people where He is calling you to meet a need.

Influence is not just what happens to your daughter; it is also what can happen through her. Are there needs around you that you've tended to ignore because you believe you're in the way, or not enough, or because you think you have to wait until your daughter is older? If so, I encourage you to change your perspective. Look for opportunities to bring your influence and your daughter into a world in need of the very thing that you both have to offer.

"You are the salt of the earth. But if the salt loses its saltiness, how can it be made salty again? It is no longer good for anything, except to be thrown out and trampled underfoot. You are the light of the world. A town built on a hill cannot be hidden. Neither do people light a lamp and put it under a bowl. Instead they put it on its stand, and it gives light to everyone in the house. In the same way, let your light shine before others, that they may see your good deeds and glorify your Father in heaven."

MATTHEW 5:13-16

———————————— LET'S PRAY ————————————

Dear God,

Thank You for the opportunities You have given me to serve You and to love others. Thank You for the influence You have given me, and the reminder that influence is a two-way street. Help me to remember that my daughter is an asset to my ability to serve the needs of the "least of these" around me, not a burden. Open my eyes to her gifts and to the needs around us so we can begin to meet them together.

I am available to You, and I offer my time, talent, and treasure to serve in whatever capacity You see fit. And I offer my daughter back to You and trust that even now You will begin to use her time, talent, and treasure for Your kingdom purposes. Lord, help her to know that You can and want to use her now, not only when she is grown. And give me the trust to let go so that You might use her in great and marvelous ways.

She is Yours, and I trust You with her.

In Jesus's name, amen.

14

HER HEART FOR OTHERS

WYNTER | In the grocery store line, on the playground, and at the car wash, my girls ask people they meet, "Are you a Christian?" It makes me smile. I love that their passion for Jesus has already ignited a fire and a boldness in their lives. It's beautiful. It challenges and encourages me, and at times it makes me really, really nervous. Can our children, and can we, become so focused on changing a person that we miss the opportunity to just love them? God does not place people in our lives as projects, but as souls that need to know His love.

My second grader came home after her third week at a new school and announced that her new friend and tablemate was not a Christian. She was distraught. She explained to me that she had been talking to her friend about being a Christian, and her friend didn't want to talk about it anymore. "But Mommy, what am I supposed to do?" she asked.

"Love her," I replied.

She looked puzzled. I could tell that my tender, caring, and cautious seven-year-old was expecting me to be a little concerned. "But Mommy," she continued, "she said she doesn't even go to church!"

"Okay, keep loving her," I replied again. I'm not sure if she was expecting me to give her a Bible verse that could convince her new friend to believe, or for me to simply tell her to abandon this new friendship completely. But I could tell from the look on her face that my advice to just love her friend was not what she was expecting.

"But in your hearts revere Christ as Lord. Always be prepared to give an answer to everyone who asks you to give the reason for the hope that you have. But do this with gentleness and respect, keeping a clear conscience, so that those who speak maliciously against your good behavior in Christ may be ashamed of their slander."

1 PETER 3:15-16

There is no denying that Christ calls us to deliver a specific message: "Repent. Believe. Be saved." However, I reminded my daughter—and myself—that Christ Himself approached saving lives from a place of love. "For God so loved the world…" (John 3:16). Even when people didn't believe and even when they no longer wanted to listen, He loved. Jesus Christ walked with people. He plopped Himself smack-dab in the middle of their lives, broke bread with them, served them, and ultimately loved them unto Himself. He never denied their need for salvation, but His love is the tool He used to speak. And it still is today. We must teach our children to do the same. *We* must do the same. After all, God is love. Without love, the message of salvation cannot exist.

How do we teach our daughters to love their unsaved friends without turning them into "projects"? Here are six ways to help our children love those who are far from the Lord.

- Invite unsaved families into our lives. Have them over to our homes for dinner or for playdates.

- Encourage our children to be an example of God's love in their actions and attitudes.

- Teach our children what it means to be a friend and the kind of person others can trust.

- Create a prayer list or jar and commit to praying together as a family for those who do not know Jesus.

- Practice selflessness. Serve others and give of ourselves, even if it means giving up something that we want.

- Teach our children to always be willing to share their hope in God. First Peter 3:15-16 is a great Scripture passage to memorize and a reminder that God has called us to be prepared to share the message of salvation through our own story. In addition to memorizing their story, have our children practice telling it to our family.

JONATHAN | Our goal is to be ambassadors for Christ and to train our girls in the job description of an ambassador.

But that brings up a question. What do ambassadors do? Well, a nation's ambassadors represent their country in a foreign land, and they have four main roles.

First, they represent their country to the host country where they live. In every way, they are the face of their home country to the watching world. With their

"Therefore, we are ambassadors for Christ, as though God were making an appeal through us; we beg you on behalf of Christ, be reconciled to God. He made Him who knew no sin to be sin on our behalf, so that we might become the righteousness of God in Him."

2 CORINTHIANS 5:20-21 NASB

voice, their dress, their conduct, and every interaction they have, they are representing not just themselves, but also their nation and its governing officials. Their goal is to have strategic interactions to further the interests of their own country and the agenda of its administration.

Second, ambassadors relay the policy stances and governing guidelines of the country they represent. It is their job to inform the host country of where they stand on every issue that might come up and to persuade the other country to see things as they do. Oftentimes this comes with attending events and creating opportunities for both sides to talk in order to make the process more natural.

Third, ambassadors are responsible for looking after and caring for their fellow citizens living as foreigners in the host country with them. As far as their country is concerned, they are responsible, meaning they are to do whatever they can within their power to make sure none of their fellow citizens are alone as they sojourn in the foreign country.

Lastly, they manage. An ambassador is rarely working alone in a foreign country and typically has at least a few others on their team. So although a lot of their job seems glamorous, this is probably the part that can seem tedious. It takes diligence and an attitude that comes out of their love for their nation. In that love they must find the motivation necessary to serve their country despite the possible danger.

Just like an ambassador for a nation, our girls have been called to represent a kingdom; Jesus called it the kingdom of God. Yes, there is only one way to enter that kingdom, and that is through repentance. But just as each individual ambassador has different gifts and abilities, so do our girls. As we encourage them to represent the King and His kingdom, may we encourage them to utilize the gifts God has given them to persuade people toward a love for both.

Like a nation's ambassador, may our girls know our policy book, the Bible, inside and out—well enough to speak to its benefits, its truth, and its rightful place in the world.

In addition to caring about those foreigners they are trying to persuade to enter the kingdom of God, may they never forget that they have a responsibility to stand with those who are a part of the kingdom already—fellow believers whom God has connected them with to love, serve, encourage, and defend.

And may they never get weary in their work, but may their love for the kingdom of God and for their King, Jesus, drive them to keep representing Him, knowing that the call He has on their lives is a noble cause.

As we think about our role in parenting our girls, and as we impress Christlikeness upon them, we realize that this job description applies to all of us. You know, ambassadors are also called diplomats, and though in our heated political culture this term can sometimes be understood negatively, a diplomat's role is to be sensitive to people while being effective.

My hope and prayer for my girls and yours is that they will be sensitive to the people and needs around them because of the Holy Spirit's work in their life, which is the first ingredient necessary to effectiveness in the kingdom of God.

———————————— LET'S PRAY ————————————

Father,

Thank You for making me an ambassador in Your kingdom and for trusting me with the message of reconciliation. May I take my responsibility to be Your representative seriously, starting in my home with my daughter. May I be reminded continually that You have not placed me here in this world to serve my own purposes but to serve Yours. Help me to live the job description You've given so that my daughter can absorb it through my life as I teach it to her, as well.

Lord, may she be so in love with Your kingdom that being an ambassador for it would be second nature. May she not get so caught up in the job description that she forgets that You have gifted her distinctively to represent You. Lord, in her friendships, in her school, in our neighborhood, and over the course of her life, use her as a beacon of light. Help her to tell her story of how she met You. When called upon, may she share that story with honesty, passion, and conviction.

May she be motivated by Your great love for her. And may her love for others be her strongest voice of Your goodness.

She is Yours, and I trust You with her.

In Jesus's name, amen.

15

HER QUESTIONS

WYNTER | If you have a daughter over the age of two years old, then I am sure you are familiar with the "why" phase. From the very beginning our girls have questions. I have been asked everything from why pinkie toes do not continue to grow to why a sister's front teeth look like popcorn kernels! I'm sure that if we were able to sit down and talk, we could create a coffee-table book of just "why" questions, though we would probably not want to add all our answers.

I've gotten used to hearing "why," but I'm still a bit apprehensive when responding. I don't know about your experience, but sometimes my kids can catch me off guard and hit me with a whopper when I least expect it.

I've learned that when my girls say, "Mommy, can I ask you a question?" the questions can often be hard to answer. From creation, to finance, to questions of biblical proportion, I can oftentimes be crippled by my lack of expertise.

Over time I've learned that when my girls say, "Mommy, I have a question," I should just brace myself because some of the questions have gotten harder. I'll never forget the time my husband and I had to begin reading a series of books that explained sex. It took everything in us to listen to the questions that her little mind wanted answers to that we just weren't ready for. Or when my daughter asked me, "Can I try on a pad?" much earlier than she needed to.

I'll just be honest; I don't like having hard conversations with my girls. It's just not my cup of tea. But even more than that, I don't like when someone else beats me to it. So despite my discomfort, I have to be willing and ready to answer the questions.

Think of it this way. When in need of groceries, do you write your grocery list while standing in the middle of the potato chip aisle, starving? It can be done, but it's probably not the wisest way to tackle the situation. You will probably leave with junk food in your cart. On the other hand, if you want to get the most out of your time and experience, you must show up to the store prepared. You look around your pantry in advance, consider your upcoming menu, and add to your list little by little as you prepare to meet a future need. There is wisdom in planning this way. Your trip is smooth and purposeful, and most importantly, you can manage to avoid the aisles of junk with their tempting and appetizing pictures, jingles, and artificial flavors. Your choices are not dictated by your cravings.

This is the way I believe we need to approach conversations with our girls. There are lists of things they need to know, and they don't necessarily need to know them all at once. Consider the future and plan accordingly. Our job is to observe, prepare, and note when it is time to put another item on the list. We don't want to wait until our girls are standing in the middle of overwhelming, enticing, unhealthy options, hoping they will make wise choices. They need to be prepared and equipped well in advance to avoid the jingles and artificial flavors. Whether they are in pre-K or high school, society will not wait for us to fill their carts if we leave them hungry. A variety of sources—peers, movies, television, music, teachers—will be ready to feed them.

Are you like me, weary of the questions and preferring to avoid having to answer? The next time she asks a question that you don't feel comfortable with or that you think can wait to be answered, assume she is going to go ask someone else. May that be your motivation, just like it was mine, to sit down and engage in the conversations, knowing that you are filling a hole that could quite possibly be filled by someone else who doesn't have your daughter's best interests at heart.

JONATHAN | With four girls in our home, I have been dumbfounded on many occasions. There is nothing worse than having a barrage of questions thrown at me, especially when I don't have the answers. But unfortunately, as our girls age, this situation becomes normal. We will sometimes feel small in the face of their difficult questions.

My oldest girl took a science class that included the study of evolution—a first for her. I knew that I questioned macroevolutionary theory pretty seriously as a Bible-believing Christian, but her questions were coming because of a video she watched at school that presented it as fact. There were a few things I could do in that situation. First, I could make something up. Fortunately for me, I didn't know enough about it to even do that and feel good about myself. Second, I could ignore her question and tell her to go back to school and let them answer. Third, I could tell her that macroevolution isn't true by saying, "Because the Bible tells me so." Lastly, I could swallow my pride and tell her, "I don't know," followed by, "Why don't we learn a little more about it together?"

Thankfully, in that situation, I made the right decision. I told her that I didn't know enough to answer her question, and I committed to looking a little deeper into the topic to explain why I thought what I thought. I challenged her to dig even deeper herself. I also had the opportunity to point her to the Bible and other scientists who would support a Christian worldview as it relates to evolution. Though I could have run away, I chose to dig in and enter her world, which gave me a bit more credibility with her when she had her next question. Saying "I don't know" doesn't make you a bad parent.

"Neither do people light a lamp and put it under a bowl. Instead they put it on its stand, and it gives light to everyone in the house."

MATTHEW 5:15

Some of the questions thrown at us have to do with exposing the tender hearts of our girls to things that are often considered shameful. Other topics will open them up to the darkness of the world around them. It's easy to avoid the scary things in our world, but avoidance disguised as protection is one of the most harmful things we can do. As Christian parents, we have to realize that discussing hard topics like sexuality, death, natural disasters, or atheism with our kids will not harm them. Instead, these difficult conversations will protect them and encourage them to ask more questions and search God's Word for themselves.

God commands us to be a light. Keeping our girls in the dark does not make the world less dark. However, it does limit their ability to shine.

Most people only think about the gospel and the fact that "Jesus loves you" when they think about Matthew 5:15, but our girls need to know that all of God's Word is good news. Everything He has to say about His goodness is light. Additionally, His Word talks a lot about darkness, and though we prefer the light, our daughters must understand the darkness and be able to discern between darkness and light.

Of course, as we answer their questions, there are some things that we need to consider as age appropriate or inappropriate, and that will differ from girl to girl based on her maturity. There are things we discussed with our firstborn daughter well ahead of our number two. And as you might have guessed having made it this far into the book, we suggest that you seek the Lord for His wisdom and discernment as you make big decisions like when to discuss sex with your daughter. Pray for wisdom so you'll be ready when a decision needs to be made in the spur of the moment.

Let's seek to grow as parents together in equipping our girls with the truth they need to guard their hearts and protect their minds. As you share, they will need to be reminded that they are never given information to judge but so that they can love the way that Christ does.

WYNTER | Do you struggle with talking to your girls about hard topics because of the darkness it exposes? Or do you hate the discomfort of it? As you think about some topics—maybe even some cultural hot-button topics—which ones make you cringe? You may need to pray about how to discuss them with your daughter.

Whatever the topic, here are a few tips to help you approach difficult conversations with your girls.

- *Seek wisdom.* Before you decide to talk with your girls, you should pray these words: "Lord, give me wisdom." We never want to plant seeds of fear, judgment, or confusion into the hearts of our children, and we need God's wisdom to lead us as we navigate truth that may seem difficult.

- *Prepare.* Know what God has to say about the topic and prepare to show your girls why you believe what you believe based on Scripture. Don't be afraid to seek out expert opinions. Doing so doesn't make you dumb. It makes you wise.

- *Be honest.* Let your girls ask questions, and regardless of your comfort level, answer them honestly using God's truth as the foundation.

- *Speak with love and seek humility.* We must always remember that as believers, we need to live a life of truth and love. We cannot have a conversation about hard truth without discussing God's love and grace.

- *Repeat.* Oftentimes a question is more than a question. Our girls will need to process some topics for more than a single conversation. You are building a relationship grounded in love and truth.

LET'S PRAY

"All Scripture is God-breathed and is useful for teaching, rebuking, correcting and training in righteousness, so that the servant of God may be thoroughly equipped for every good work."

2 TIMOTHY 3:16-17

Father,

Thank You for giving me the role of lead voice in my daughter's life. Thank You for allowing me to herald the truth with love and grace. Continually remind me that all of Your Word is available as I seek to bring clarity to my daughter's world. Lord, help me to answer the questions that she voices, and give me the insight to read into the questions weighing heavy on her mind.

I pray that when she has a question,

I will be the first person she thinks to ask, and I ask that You would help me to be prepared. When I'm not prepared, remind me that it's okay to say, "I don't know," and give me the vitality to seek out the answers. Give me confidence in Your Word and the strength I need to discuss anything and everything with my daughter. And may You be her ultimate source of answers, utilizing me as Your representative and others that You bring along to assist.

She is Yours, and I trust You with her.

Amen.

16

HER COURAGE

JONATHAN | I've been afraid of flying for as long as I can remember. I can't say it's for lack of experience. I fly multiple times a month and have done so for the past 12 years. My career has taken me all over the United States. I've flown on big planes, small planes, tiny planes, prop planes, and on rare occasions, private planes.

If you ask anyone who's traveled with me, they could tell you that I'm about as nervous a flyer as you can find. Sweaty palms, firm grip, startled looks…and the list goes on and on.

It's only gotten worse with each of my girls' births. It seems as if the reality of raising my girls has changed the intensity of my fears. Not to be morbid, but it used to be the simple thought of my plane going down and me being alive to experience it. But more recently I've been afraid of not seeing my girls again. I worry about who would raise them and who would protect them.

For a nervous flyer, one of the most exciting things that can happen after boarding a plane is realizing that there is an off-duty pilot seated within view. He's not in control and is subject to the on-duty pilots in the cockpit. He's in the same position as me, but there's something about his presence that just calms me down and gives me a bit of courage. When I know he's there, I literally can't take my eyes off him for too long. When the bird takes off, you know exactly where I'm looking. When the pilot comes on over the loudspeaker, I'm watching the off-duty pilot's facial expressions. When we hit a bump, I look to see if he lifts the brim of his pilot's cap that is tilted over his eyes as he takes a nap. And as we land, my eyes typically rotate from my view out of my window toward him again.

"Have no fear of sudden disaster or of the ruin that overtakes the wicked, for the Lord will be at your side and will keep your foot from being snared."

PROVERBS 3:25-26

I'm not exaggerating. It's been bad, but some time ago the Lord convicted me over my irrational fears. You see, in all my 12 years of flying, I've never seen the off-duty pilot flinch. I've never seen one get emotionally stirred or concerned about whether the pilots in the cockpit knew what they were doing. They sit there, simply trusting that the on-duty pilots have been trained, just like them, to handle their business in the calm and in the storm.

I don't even remember how I stumbled upon the Scripture passage above, but it hasn't left my side since the first day I read it.

I'm sure I'd read this passage before. Probably many times. But the conviction I felt this time was life-giving. I realized that my fear was a direct offense to God. I was made aware that God's expectation of me, even command, was that I not fear. I knew I fell woefully short of this command in this specific area.

I decided to commit this Scripture passage to memory. So as the plane took off, I simply began to recite the verses in my mind. Literally, over and over again. On one particular flight, I was flying west over the Rocky Mountains. I don't fully understand why, but flying over mountains typically creates more turbulence. I know it has something to do with the warm and cold air, but other than that, I have not retained the explanation. This flight held up to what I had been told many times before.

So I recited the Scripture verses over and over again, pausing to pray between recitations, asking God to make this passage my reality. Over time He did, taking Proverbs 3:25-26 deep down into my soul.

The beauty of my experience was that God personalized that Scripture passage to me. He helped me to see that He, being at my side, was just like the off-duty pilot sitting in eyesight. I slowly began to trust His Word, leaning on His past faithfulness in my life. I began to fly with a bit more confidence. Now, as I fly alongside my wife, who happens to be a nervous flyer as well, my courage and confidence in God can be a sort of strength to her as well as to my girls, a few of whom inherited the nervous-flyer gene.

I would be stretching the truth if I said I don't have moments of fear. But I have a growing confidence in the faithfulness of God. I'm learning to turn my face from the off-duty pilot to the ultimate Pilot. Of course, that's the beauty of God. He's in the seat beside me, and He's in the cockpit. Through His Holy Spirit and through His Word, I get to experience Him much closer than I do the off-duty pilot. It's there that He quiets my spirit and reminds me that He's flying the plane of my life as well.

When I think of fear, I remember Joshua in the Old Testament. Joshua was God's man after Moses. If you've never done it before, I recommend you read the books of Deuteronomy and Joshua. These books speak specifically to the leadership of Moses and Joshua. They were two very different leaders, but both of them had to face their fears.

Moses had taken the people as far as he could, and then he died. It was time to turn over the keys to the next generation, and Joshua was at the helm. Joshua had big shoes to fill and two gigantic problems along the way! First, he wasn't Moses. Moses had proven his leadership ability and miraculously had taken the people from

"Now Joshua son of Nun was filled with the spirit of wisdom because Moses had laid his hands on him."

DEUTERONOMY 34:9

captivity in Egypt after more than 400 years. Joshua was merely Moses's assistant.

Second, the Lord had promised to take the people of Israel to the Promised Land. But the Promised Land was inhabited by large groups of people, many of whom were prepared to fight and annihilate Joshua and the nation of Israel.

Joshua was nervous, I'm sure. Afraid, overwhelmed, and probably anxious. God knew it from the very beginning. He wasn't surprised. So He did two things. First, He filled Joshua with His Spirit. You can read about this in the last chapter of Deuteronomy.

In other words, God made His presence even more available to Joshua, much like my off-duty pilot.

Second, He gave Joshua the single greatest reason not to be afraid.

> No one will be able to stand against you all the days of your life. As I was with Moses, so I will be with you; I will never leave you nor forsake you. Be strong and courageous, because you will lead these people to inherit the land I swore to their ancestors to give them.

> Be strong and very courageous. Be careful to obey all the law my servant Moses gave you; do not turn from it to the right or to the left, that you may be successful wherever you go. Keep this Book of the Law always on your lips; meditate on it day and night, so that you may be careful to do everything written in it. Then you will be prosperous and successful. Have I not commanded you? Be strong and courageous. Do not be afraid; do not be discouraged, for the Lord your God will be with you wherever you go (Joshua 1:5-9).

Three times in the verses above, God commands Joshua not to be afraid. He actually tells him to do the exact opposite of being afraid. He tells him to be strong and courageous. Each time He says it with a different emphasis.

First, God tells Joshua that He will lead him and that He will give him success. He essentially guarantees him success, giving Joshua a vision for what success would look like. It included God's promises from the past that had been fulfilled. Joshua had just watched Moses lead the people out of bondage and captivity. God was reminding him of past victory to give him confidence for victory in the future.

Second, God tells Joshua to stay in the Book of the Law. He tells him to meditate on His Word and reminded him that his success would come as he honored the Lord. He wanted to show Joshua the integrity, purity, and holiness that would be required to achieve lasting success, and God knew that Joshua's confidence would rise and fall based on his commitment to the truth found in the Book of the Law.

But on the third occasion, God changes His tune. He makes His last statement in the form of a question, almost as if to say, "Look, buddy, are you going to trust Me on this one?" It's here that He gives him the greatest news of all!

God gave Joshua a vision, and He reminded Joshua of His standard. Saving the best for last, He didn't want Joshua to think that he was going it alone.

WYNTER | As I think about my girls and the future world they are inheriting and the tasks that God will be calling them to, I get a bit nervous. I think about all the possible traps, enemies, and pitfalls they will encounter, and I get a bit anxious,

"Have I not commanded you? Be strong and courageous. Do not be afraid; do not be discouraged, for the LORD your God will be with you wherever you go."
JOSHUA 1:9

even paralyzed sometimes. I think about selfish boys who are only interested in their own pleasure. I think about girlfriends who will try to drag my girls along for a ride down Drama Street. And I think about all the potential circumstances in life that loom with each day: sickness, rebellion, and evil. It can be a bit overwhelming.

But there is much hope!

I'm 100 percent sure that God has a vision and a plan for my girls' lives, just as He did for Joshua.

I'm praying that my girls meditate on God's Word day and night, just like God encouraged Joshua to do.

But most encouraging to me is knowing that just as the Lord was with Joshua, He will be with my girls wherever they go. I can't be there all the time, but God will be! When my little girl is afraid, I know that she can turn to her Rock. He will never leave her and is walking with her in every situation she walks into. Cognitively, I know and believe that, but experientially I'm still walking that faith out one day at a time. So I pray for courage—for her and for me— and I tell myself that my proximity to our loving God and His Word will make all the difference in the world.

I also think back on God's faithfulness in my life. He literally saved my mother and used her influence to bring me into relationship with Him. I watched my mother walk with courage as a single mom, trusting that the God who redeemed her life would also redeem her circumstances. Moses told the Israelites, "The Lord your God will restore your fortunes" (Deuteronomy 30:3), and He has surely done that for my mother.

God took a young girl (me) who was growing up on some of the toughest city streets in our nation and walked her all the way to where she is now. The Israelites questioned God about their journey to the Promised Land, and I would have questioned God too if He had shared His plan back then. He didn't, but in retrospect, my life is a constant reminder of His faithfulness. As I lead my daughters, it gives me courage. What He has already done for me is the very ammunition I need to encourage them in the Lord in every season and circumstance.

What about you? Are there areas in your life that are causing you anxiety and worry? Are you constantly thinking about what can go wrong in your daughter's life? Are you taking your eyes off the one who will give you both courage? If so, take this moment to reaffirm your trust in God's faithfulness. I would even encourage you to use the books of Deuteronomy and Joshua in your time with the Lord to remember what He has done in the past, and pray that He would bring that same Word alive for your future.

I would also encourage you to take some time soon to sit with your daughter and share one thing in your life that God did for you when you were in a no-win situation or when you needed courage the most. Tell her how God brought you through it and remind her that He will do the same thing in her life. And most importantly, lay your fears, worries, and anxieties at the foot of the cross, exchanging them for confidence and courage in the Lord.

——————————— LET'S PRAY ———————————

Father,

You have given me a clear command in Your Word to not be afraid. You've reminded me that regardless of my circumstances and regardless of what lies ahead, You are with me. May I stand confident with courage in my heart, knowing that You are near.

Just as the people of Israel saw Joshua marching into battle with courage and were encouraged themselves, may my life be one that is courage on display. May I signal to my daughter that You can be trusted. In every place that she sets her foot, may she do so knowing that she doesn't walk alone, but that Your very real and powerful presence is with her and in her.

And when she walks into circumstances that require her to make a bold stand for You, may she do so with the courage and confidence that comes only from an intimate relationship with You.

She is Yours, and I trust You with her.

In Jesus's name, amen.

"No one will be able to stand against you all the days of your life. As I was with Moses, so I will be with you; I will never leave you nor forsake you. Be strong and courageous, because you will lead these people to inherit the land I swore to their ancestors to give them.

"Be strong and very courageous. Be careful to obey all the law my servant Moses gave you; do not turn from it to the right or to the left, that you may be successful wherever you go. Keep this Book of the Law always on your lips; meditate on it day and night, so that you may be careful to do everything written in it. Then you will be prosperous and successful. Have I not commanded you? Be strong and courageous. Do not be afraid; do not be discouraged, for the LORD your God will be with you wherever you go."

JOSHUA 1:5-9

17

HER HUSBAND

JONATHAN | Every year we do it. It started off when our oldest daughter was seven, and the tradition has continued every year since then. It began with our firstborn, and then we added our second. A few years later our twins joined their sisters on the journey.

I'm talking about overnight summer camp. As we've mentioned previously, each year we drop off all four of them, and we have an empty house for seven days! We literally don't know what to do with ourselves, so we do nothing! Seven days of nothing.

"You want some sushi for lunch, babe?"

"Sure!"

"How about a movie?"

"Sure!"

"You want to watch another movie?"

"Sure!"

"I don't feel like cooking. Do you want to eat out for dinner?"

"Sure!"

"How about dessert?"

You can probably guess the answer. We rarely have a time when all four girls are out of our home, so we cherish this time to relax, get to know each other again, and rest from all the activities that come with parenting four girls.

The more we do it the easier it gets, but it hasn't always been this way.

I remember our very first step—choosing the right camp. We were pretty uncertain. We did everything we could do to make sure that we were leaving our daughter in the care of a summer camp that was safe, and one that we hoped would be the best fit for her. Living in Texas, we had a few great options. At the center of the Bible Belt, there are numerous opportunities to make sure that your child has an opportunity to grow in a relationship with the Lord. Thankfully, we knew of a host of summer camps with awesome reputations.

But still, this was our firstborn daughter! We were not going to take any risk in the process of finding the right match. But we had to make a choice, and choose we did. We ended up choosing the camp with a great reputation and one that we knew was vetted by several of our friends and family.

I remember the weeks leading up to her departure. As parents, we were doing all we could to prepare. We were both a bit anxious, for a few different reasons. Now, I know chapter 16 was about doing away with fear in exchange for courage, but don't judge me! I'm a work in progress! First, we were anxious about the thought of dropping off our little girl. We questioned whether we were making the right decision and whether she would be able to make it without us.

The other anxiety had to do with our preparation. We wondered whether we had prepared her emotionally. Even at seven, she still had emotional breakdowns and difficulties that we routinely helped her through. We wondered, "What will she do without us guiding her through those moments each day? Will she eat right? Will she

bathe? Do we feel good about her ability to swim?" Our worries
seemed to be never ending.

In addition to that anxiety came the sheer physical anxiety of
preparing her for that day when we would pack her up and ship her
off. Unless you've done youth summer camp, it's difficult to imagine. First, there's the trunk. A significant investment, to say the least.

Second, comes purchasing 80 percent of the things they want
you to put in the trunk. Flashlights, bug spray, water shoes, theme-
night outfits. The list goes on and on. Then there is adding the 80
percent new with the 20 percent that you already own but you had
to find in her closet and dresser and under her bed.

Lastly, there is putting each outfit and item in its own ziplock
bag. Everything was labeled and placed in the trunk. (This may not
be not so necessary for boys, but for girls—how could we not!) The
task is physically exhausting and emotionally draining. Did I mention that Wynter has done this job since the very beginning? I can
describe it so well because I've watched her every year for several
years, but thankfully, the Lord has spared me from this part of it!

Choosing and preparing were difficult, but those stressors
couldn't hold a candle to the very moment we have been preparing
for—the drop-off!

It began with fear, knowing that we had no control over our firstborn daughter's life for the next seven days. I thought about the person who would be responsible for her—her counselor. I questioned
how I could trust this person we had just met. And before I knew it,
I was kissing my daughter goodbye.

Next came sadness. I remember as my wife and I drove off after
kissing her goodbye. I was a bit somber, and Wynter was crying. We
got in the car and drove away quietly. It was a new and empty feeling. We didn't have a lot of family living around us in Texas, so our
girls rarely left our side for more than a few hours.

It was in this moment that we said a prayer. We had no control and no oversight, and we simply concluded that we had to trust the Lord. I grabbed Wynter's hand, pretending to be tough, and led her in a prayer of trusting the Lord to protect Alena. To protect her from herself and to protect her from others that we didn't know. To help her get clean in the shower and to help her brush her teeth. To make sure she didn't devour too much junk and that she ate plenty of nutritious food.

But while all these prayers were serious, we quickly realized that she was in the Lord's hands. In that moment, we were giving her back to Him, knowing that He was all she had.

We found hope in that thought. We remembered that the Lord is all she has ever really had. Yes, we were her caretakers and the stewards that God was using to train, discipline, love, and grow her, but ultimately, she had never really left His arms.

Driving home, we settled in to the fact that the Lord had this in His plans all along. He purposed for her to go. He actually picked the camp, though we thought it was our vetting process. He provided us with the resources necessary and all the supplies needed for the journey. He would make sure that she was well taken care of all week, and He would give her joy. Ultimately, He would be the one to meet her at camp and surround her with His love.

Having done this for many years now, we don't have the same fears and anxieties and worries we had before. Yes, there is always a bit of nervousness, knowing they are a few hours away and that life circumstances are inevitable, but we don't do it with the same energy.

We've come to enjoy the season. The quiet. We've come to enjoy the role that God gives us during that week of just trusting Him with her.

With each year that I drop my daughters off, I feel as though I'm in full dress rehearsal for the inevitable handoff that I will make for each of my girls one day, Lord willing. Eventually I'll be dropping them off for much longer than seven days—I'm talking about handing them off to their husbands.

Although I'll be involved in the process of choosing, I won't be the sole decision maker. I'm sure I'll have the same trust issues that I had with the camp counselor, but a thousand times greater! Prayerfully, I'll have more than a few minutes to meet, vet, and grow in relationship with the man that I'll be entrusting her to. The preparation is much more intense than getting her ready for camp, and unfortunately, there is no simple checklist.

I can't imagine how real the feelings will be. Fear, I'm sure. Anxiety, a given.

But there's one big difference between camp and my daughters' future husbands and families. With camp, we put the trunks away each year and forget about them until a few weeks prior to camp the next year. With her future husband, I never stop preparing.

Everything we are doing is preparation for that day. We disciple them with this in mind. I strive to treat my wife with Christlike love so they can see it modeled. And I enjoy them even more in the short window of time we have with them at home.

WYNTER | I've prayed for them since before they were born. Simple prayers, yes. But prayers of hope. Hope that my girls' futures will be bright. Hope that my sons-in-law will be responsible, godly men.

Often, I find myself praying for four people I have never met. These unknown figures play a significant role in the future of my family, and I will one day entrust them with pieces of my heart.

I pray for my sons-in-law as if they were mine because one day they will be. Here's what I pray.

──────────────── LET'S PRAY ────────────────

Dear God,

There is a young man somewhere that I probably have never met. He is playing on a playground, sitting at a dining room table, or throwing rocks into a pond.

To be honest, I have no idea what he is doing, what his life looks like (or his face for that matter), who his family is, or what his values are. But I am dedicated to lifting him up to You.

This young man will one day marry my daughter.

As tears roll down my cheeks, I cry out to You to bless, protect, and direct his life.

I pray that You would surround him with Your love. Place people in his life that will lay a foundation of Your truth, Your love, and Your values.

Keep him safe. Keep him pure. Make him Yours.

Even now, I pray that You would prepare a love in him for his future wife and cause this love to drive his actions.

Make him sensitive to Your voice. Make him eager to seek You and to seek the plan You have for his life.

Teach him to lay down his life for You. Prepare him to one day lay it down for my daughter and their children. Teach him to lead by following You.

Lord, I trust Your plan for their lives together, and I anticipate their union and the glory it will bring to Your kingdom.

He is Yours, and I trust You with him.

In Jesus's name, amen.

18

HER PATH

WYNTER | The older my children get, the more I realize just how little control I have over the testimony and story that God is creating in their lives. With each lesson they learn, He is answering my prayers, and He is teaching me to trust Him for their futures.

My biggest fears and my biggest desires somehow seem to be wrapped into one, and I am learning to trust God with both.

If there is one thing the parenting journey has taught me, it's this: Parenting is just as much about my relationship with Christ right now as it is about training my children for their future.

It's in the moments of watching my children suffer, sacrifice, and serve that I am truly challenged. Heartbreak, discomfort, and pain are very real parts of raising Christlike children.

Tears may roll down the sweet cheeks of our little girls. There will be times when their good decisions will break their hearts. But in these moments, realize that the test may very well be yours. Will you trust God with your daughters, or will you protect and shield them from the need to practice the Word you've taught them?

I can remember sitting in the back of a room and witnessing my six-year-old daughter showing a level of humility that would make a parent proud. Yet surprisingly, the experience left me feeling unprepared for the possibility of answered prayers. Here's what happened.

A young man on the stage at a youth worship service asked, "Can I have four volunteers?"

Immediately, all over the room, hands were flailing, bodies were jumping, and kids were screaming, "ME! ME! ME!"

The young man on stage loosely pointed to different areas around the room and called out, "You! You! You! You!"

About seven kids came running down the aisle, climbed the stairs, and planted their bodies within inches of the man, anticipating what was to come. My daughter was one of them.

The young man looked down at the kids and said, "We have too many volunteers. I need three of you to go back to your seats."

I watched my daughter, with a smile on her face, immediately turn around and bounce back to her seat. After a little prodding, two more kids left the stage.

I should have been proud of her leadership, her decision, her attitude, and her obedience, right? After all, these are the very attributes that I'd been praying for her since she was born.

But can I be honest?

My immediate feelings were not that of a proud mother. Instead, I felt sad for her and a bit disturbed by the selfishness of the other kids. I wanted her to have something that I knew she wanted. But all I could do was watch quietly from afar as she humbly surrendered and took her seat.

Although I know that sacrifice is at the center of Christlike living, the reality of the disappointment caused by her godly decision left me feeling empty. It's one thing to teach and encourage our kids to give up their desires for the benefit of another and to be kind to those who mistreat them, but it's an entirely different ball game to sit on the sidelines and witness it happening.

As hard as it is for me to watch, I do pray that they want Jesus even when it costs them something. I want them to love God more—more than they love me, our family, and their comfort. And more than they love the dreams that I can conjure up.

Having shared this story, I feel the need to confess and come clean. I have a problem. Okay, well, I have several. But this is one that directly relates to this conversation.

The problem is that I want my daughters to have everything that God has for them, and as a parent, that can be a scary thought.

This confession can seem to be a bit of a contradiction, but let's just be honest. While my natural inclination is to protect my daughters from anything remotely close to pain, I know that a part of that journey will include pain at some level. Jesus Himself, the holy Son of God, suffered, so why should we expect less? In fact, Scripture points us to this very promise.

Is suffering what I am asking for? Absolutely not. But can you think of one of God's children who never suffered in some form for the sake of being His?

I guess what I am saying is that I fear my girls will actually walk the path and cross the bridge that leads to God's perfect will in their lives, and sometimes that may be hard for me to watch.

Here are a few ways that Jesus Christ, our Savior and Lord, suffered.

- *He was betrayed.* "Judas, are you betraying the Son of Man with a kiss?" (Luke 22:48).

- *He was rejected.* "'Which of the two do you want me to release for you?' asked the governor. 'Barabbas,' they answered. 'What shall I do, then, with Jesus who is called the Messiah?' Pilate asked. They all answered, 'Crucify him!'" (Matthew 27:21-22).

- *He was teased.* "And kneeling before him, they mocked him, saying, 'Hail, King of the Jews!' And they spit on him and took the reed and struck him on the head" (Matthew 27:29-30 ESV).

- *He was spat upon.* "Then they spit in his face and struck him. And some slapped him, saying 'Prophesy to us, you Christ! Who is it that struck you?'" (Matthew 26:67-68 ESV).

- *He was deserted.* "Then all the disciples left him and fled" (Matthew 26:56 ESV).

Get the picture? If all these things happened to Jesus, then I have to brace myself for the fact that some of them may happen to my girls. Following Him is not always an easy, comfortable, and rewarding journey (in the immediate).

I often ask myself if I am truly prepared to allow His will to be fully accomplished in their lives because I am 100 percent sure that what God has for them looks little like the life I want for them. Following Jesus comes at a cost. If we truly want to be committed to raising daughters who know who they are and whose they are, then we have to be prepared to pay the price.

But we can have hope in this: God has many promises for our girls. Here are a few.

- *Peace.* "Peace I leave with you; my peace I give you. I do not give to you as the world gives. Do not let your hearts be troubled and do not be afraid" (John 14:27).

- *Joy.* "Truly, truly, I say to you, you will weep and lament, but the world will rejoice. You will be sorrowful, but your sorrow will turn into joy" (John 16:20 ESV).

- *Hope.* "For to this end we toil and strive, because we have our hope set on the living God, who is the Savior of all people, especially of those who believe" (1 Timothy 4:10 ESV).

- *Forgiveness.* "If we confess our sins, he is faithful and just to forgive us our sins and to cleanse us from all unrighteousness" (1 John 1:9 ESV).

- *Everlasting love.* "See what kind of love the Father has given to us, that we should be called children of God; and so we are" (1 John 3:1 ESV).

- *Eternal life.* "For God so loved the world, that he gave his only Son, that whoever believes in him should not perish but have eternal life" (John 3:16 ESV).

> "He leads me in paths of righteousness for his name's sake."
>
> **PSALM 23:3** ESV

God's plan may not look like the one I have conjured up and tucked away in my heart, but ultimately I pray that He will continually give me glimpses of our daughters living their faith out loud in the form of sacrifice, humility, and selflessness. Along with that prayer, I pray that He will prepare me for the journey that He has for their lives.

JONATHAN | When I think about the path that God has for my little girls, I am reminded of Psalm 23:3.

I often forget that God is purposefully guiding my daughters along His paths, but He gave me a wonderful reminder that started with these words: "Babe, we just got invited on a trip to Israel. It leaves in three weeks."

Wynter was speaking of a trip that she and my oldest daughter Alena (12 years old at the time) were invited on while they were speaking together at a local event in Dallas. The man who invited them (seemingly at random) was speaking on the same stage with them at the time. He was working on behalf of another organization to book 25 "people of influence" to make a nine-day journey to the Promised Land. A few days prior to the event, two females had backed out of the trip, so while he was speaking alongside Wynter and Alena, finding two replacement "influencers" was top of mind for him. He would later tell us that his first thought was, "Man, it sure would be great to have a young influencer like Alena on this trip," knowing Alena's background with the film *War Room*.

His second thought was, "But there's no way she can go on this trip as a 12-year-old girl by herself." Minutes later he would watch her mother, whom he had neither met nor heard of, take the stage at this event. He realized that she carried "influence" of her own with her ministry to young girls, For Girls Like You. He later told me that he scrambled onto their social media pages and within minutes had made a decision that he would invite them to replace the two women who canceled. He asked them on the spot if they would go to Israel…without even asking the most important man in their lives! He then applied a little pressure and told them they had about 48 hours to decide!

The first time Wynter told me, I basically ignored her. I thought, "Who gets invited to Israel three weeks before a trip and even thinks about going?" My second thought was, "Well, things like this are starting to happen more often…"

I was starting to get used to God opening some doors that had once seemed impossible.

For example, as I think about Alena's life, I realize that there's so much that God has for her. Her life has been like an amplifier for Wynter and me in regard to all four of our girls and God's plan and path for them. God has begun to open up paths and doorways that we didn't think were even options. It's as though we had our thoughts on what God wanted to do with our girls, and then He interjected a thought that was nowhere on our radar.

Alena getting the role in *War Room* was one of these moments. The consequent book series, Lena in the Spotlight, that would follow and that she would collaborate on with her mother was another.

This invite to go on an all-expenses-paid trip to Israel was icing on the cake.

You're probably thinking. "I can't identify with that. My daughter has not been in a movie, and she doesn't have any books. Let's be real!"

I could think the same thing myself. Remember, I have three more girls that are on different journeys. Each one is on her own path. There's no doubt in my mind that each path that God has for my girls (His daughters) is unique. I've seen that in my own family and with my own girls.

But for whatever reason, God has chosen this path for Alena. Just to be clear, Wynter and I don't cherish this path for her any more than we cherish the path that He has for our three younger girls. We anticipate watching what God will do in their lives just the same. And just as with Alena, we are watching it unfold every day.

I think about my second daughter, Kaitlyn, who had a patch of struggles in fourth-grade math. We watched the enemy try to put stumbling blocks in front of her, and then we watched the Spirit of God rise up and claim the last word. We had just reached the end of our ability to help her when God stepped in and created a custom path forward.

At the middle of every semester, we have parent-teacher conferences. Just prior to Kaitlyn's parent-teacher conference, we attended one for her younger twin sisters, Camryn and Olivia. We were pleased to know of the twins' achievements during their conference, but Kaitlyn's acute struggle was at the forefront of our minds. Somehow Kaitlyn was inserted into the conversation, and though the twin's teacher had never met Kaitlyn, she started to ask some probing questions about Kaitlyn and her struggles.

Without hesitation, and for no apparent reason other than the generosity of God, this teacher offered to tutor Kaitlyn once a week after school. We knew this required extra time and sacrifice on her part. Somewhat stunned, we accepted her offer.

They fell in love from the very first tutoring session. I can't tell you what a blessing it was to watch God provide a path we never saw. After the first week of tutoring, the teacher asked if we would be willing to leave Kaitlyn with her two afternoons a week! She doubled down! She saw Kaitlyn responding to her sessions but saw an opportunity to move faster. We of course accepted her offer and thanked the Lord Jesus for His provision.

As I continue to think about how good God was in this scenario, I'm reminded that God's path was tailor-made for our family. Kaitlyn would be tutored at our school while her older sister was in volleyball practice, and it wouldn't add a single new responsibility to our plate.

You better believe we praised God. We prayed just as loudly and fervently as when her older sister landed the role in *War Room*!

Now, what do a free trip to Israel and a generous and selfless teacher have in common? Nothing at first glance, but to Wynter and me, they represent God's shepherd-like leading. He led two of our girls down their different paths but with the same care and customization.

All of my daughters are God's children, His sheep. His Word is clear that He is leading them down unique paths—possibly paths that I would not have chosen for them.

God has very specific, customized plans for your daughter. His care is certain and real. He is working everything together—the good and the bad, and even the ugly—for her good. He wants to prosper her, and though you might not always understand, you only need to trust Him and the road He is paving for her.

When it hurts to watch, trust Him. When you don't understand, trust Him. When you don't fully understand where the path is leading, trust Him. He is clearing the path that He meant for her to walk.

—————————— LET'S PRAY ——————————

Heavenly Father,

I too often forget that You are the Shepherd who guides me. And it is sometimes difficult for me to trust that You are the Shepherd who guides my daughter.

Lord, when I forget, remind me. Remind me that You are the one who opens doors, closes doors, and puts her feet on firm ground. Remind me that though You long to use me, You don't need me, and that the plans You have for my daughter do not depend on my ability. Lord, when You want to take her down a path to teach her, help me to stay out of Your way and recognize Your hand.

Lord, give me the strength to watch You lead her without interfering. Help me to know when to step in and when to stand aside.

She is Yours, and I trust You with her.

In Jesus's name, amen.

HER RELATIONSHIP WITH THE WORLD AROUND HER—FINAL THOUGHTS

There are many sources and voices that are currently speaking into your daughter's world and mind, and they are only growing in source and content with each passing day. As parents, our responsibility is to be the primary influence in our daughter's life, having a voice over every other influence. As she considers how to spend her time, manage her friendships, and face her struggles, we should be walking with her, providing a constant voice for truth.

Conversations with our girls can be very hard for many reasons, but remember that as her parents, we are called to prepare the way. This often means pushing past our discomfort and personal agendas in order to connect her world with God's perspective. Ultimately, you are God's most influential asset in her life. Her gifts, passion, and dreams will shape her future. Are you owning your role and leveraging your influence now to prepare her for the path that He is laying ahead?

Think About It

1. How would you rate your listening skills? Does your daughter have your ear?

2. Does your daughter have a biblical understanding of friendship? How are you contributing to it?

3. What decisions have you made recently to prioritize and nurture your daughter spiritually?

4. In what ways are you attempting to cultivate your daughter's heart to serve?

5. How much time do you invest in meaningful and ongoing conversations with your daughter?

6. Are you talking to God now about her future? Her husband? Her calling? Her path?

19

KEEP GOING

WYNTER | When my oldest two girls, Alena and Kaitlyn, were very young, our days would be strategically planned around naptime, and bedtime would be deliberately and swiftly executed. We enjoyed our days together and played hard, but we had definitive boundaries and a system of shut-eye! Then something happened. Enter my third and fourth daughters—Camryn and Olivia, my twins.

We welcomed these beautiful girls into our world at once, but apparently they missed the memo about nighttime. Even though my new babies were angels...They. Would. Not. Sleep! It was not pretty.

I called for help. Yes, I did. In my desperation, I reached out to a "baby sleep expert."

She requested our current sleep schedule and then provided me a revised plan that was guaranteed to help us regain normalcy, well-rested children, and peace-filled days. The new routine required me to adjust our already strategic sleeping schedule. She prescribed intentionality and exactness to ensure the success of the program. This required waking my sleeping children at precise times to ensure they would be ready to rest again when it was time.

Do you see the dilemma? As I mentioned previously, sleep is a big deal for me, and I didn't particularly like to wake sleeping children. Especially a set of twins who were already not sleeping with any regularity! Several conversations with the "baby sleep expert" gave me courage to begin the program in hopes that scheduling down to the minute would result in two sleeping babies, two happy big sisters, and an overjoyed mommy and daddy.

Reluctantly, I tried. And tried. And tried. For a few weeks that felt like an eternity, I would lay my girls down for a certain amount of time and keep them awake for the designated time. The intention was to train them to sleep at night with adequate nap times during the day. I needed this to work, and frankly, it didn't. I was definitely doing more waking up than they were sleeping, and I was miserable. My efforts were not paying off, and I was exhausted.

In a final attempt, I reached out to my "expert" and shared our trials with her. I informed her that I was at the end of my journey with this experiment. I thanked her for her efforts and time, but just before we finished our conversation, she said a few words that are now locked into my memory. "Keep following the schedule as if it were working, because it will work." I am not sure why these words hit me so hard, but they did. I began our conversation with the intention of giving up, but I ended our talk with a brand-new drive, determination, and perspective.

A few more days went by with me putting down wide-awake babies and waking up barely sleeping babies. I was working—hard, I may add—as if the plan were working...until one day, finally, it did! One morning I woke up rested from a full night's sleep, and so did they.

JONATHAN | Maybe you've felt this way—as if you've poured all your blood, sweat, and tears into something day after day with no result in sight. Maybe you started this book exhausted and were ready to give up. Maybe there is a particular stage that you have been praying will end. Or maybe you are committed to the process, but like us, you sometimes have little faith that it will work in the end.

Well, I want to encourage you today with the same words that encouraged Wynter...

Keep _____ as if it were working, because it will work!

Fill in your blank. It may be...

    trusting that God has your daughter's heart

    believing that God is working all things together for your good

    loving beyond what you feel like you have the capacity to do

    disciplining as if it is making a difference

    encouraging, knowing that you are your daughter's greatest human asset

    guiding with the Lord as your pilot

    praying as if your parenting journey depends on it, because it does

Friends, we encourage you to keep going with your daughter as if it's working. God promises that one day it will, and I pray that you will walk in the full confidence that comes only from knowing God is with you and your daughter on this journey.

———————————————— LET'S PRAY ————————————————

Dear God,

I release my daughter into Your care.

> I surrender my desire to control her.
> I surrender my desire to manipulate her future.
> I surrender my tendency to overprotect, shelter, and suffocate her.
> I surrender my desire to be her best friend, first.
> I surrender my own dreams for her.
> I surrender my need to be her source.

She is Yours.

I'm totally open to You, dependent on You, and desperate for You to be in control as I let go. I'm relying on the fact that You are God, and that You have created my daughter for Your purpose, for this time.

> I pray that You will draw her to yourself.
> I pray that she will delight in You.
> I pray that You be will be patient with her.
> I pray that You will provide for her.
> I pray that You will bless her.
> I pray that You will use her to be a blessing to others.
> I pray that You will mature her.
> Ultimately, I pray that she shows Jesus in her very being.

I trust in Your sovereignty. I wait in expectation for Your providence.

She is Yours, and I trust You with her.

Amen.

"Therefore, brothers and sisters, since we have confidence to enter the Most Holy Place by the blood of Jesus, by a new and living way opened for us through the curtain, that is, his body, and since we have a great priest over the house of God, let us draw near to God with a sincere heart and with the full assurance that faith brings, having our hearts sprinkled to cleanse us from a guilty conscience and having our bodies washed with pure water. Let us hold unswervingly to the hope we profess, for he who promised is faithful. And let us consider how we may spur one another on toward love and good deeds, not giving up meeting together, as some are in the habit of doing, but encouraging one another—and all the more as you see the Day approaching."

HEBREWS 10:19-25

FOR GIRLS LIKE YOU

Magazine

Speak Love with
ANNIE DOWNS

FRANCESCA
BATTISTELLI

Meet 13 year old
MALLORY!
Founder of
Project Yesu

CRAFTS, RECIPES & FUN!

For Girls Like You

Wynter Pitts is the founder of For Girls Like You, a ministry to young girls and their parents that also includes a quarterly print magazine, journal, and other print and online resources.

At For Girls Like You, we have a passion and drive to introduce young girls to Christian values in a way that they are able to understand and digest so they can walk passionately and boldly in who God has created them to be.

We are dedicated to exposing girls to all the things they love (travel, positive role models, creative projects, and more) without the negative messages, imagery, and advertising that often appear in mainstream entertainment. We want every article, interview, and photo to support a Christ-centered system for our young girls!

Each issue of *For Girls Like You* is fun and colorful, featuring contributions and interviews from familiar faces as well as everyday girls who are choosing to live and shine for Christ. From designing clothing to researching biblical principles, this magazine supports parents' efforts to raise beautiful and healthy daughters whose identity is wrapped up in the love of Jesus.

For more information or to subscribe to the magazine, visit
www.forgirlslikeyou.com

To learn more about Harvest House books and
to read sample chapters, visit our website:

www.harvesthousepublishers.com

HARVEST HOUSE PUBLISHERS
EUGENE, OREGON